SQUINT

BRIEF BOOKS FOR A BUSY WORLD
Look More Closely

DONALD TRUMP

THE RHETORIC

OLIVER JONES

 EYEWEAR PUBLISHING

First published in 2016
by Eyewear Publishing Ltd
Suite 333, 19-21 Crawford Street
Marylebone, London W1H 1PJ
United Kingdom

Typeset with graphic design by Edwin Smet
Author photograph by Devyn Maher
Trump pictures Creative Commons license
Printed in England by TJ International Ltd, Padstow, Cornwall

ISBN 978-1-908998-93-4

Eyewear wishes to thank Jonathan Wonham for his generous patronage of our press.

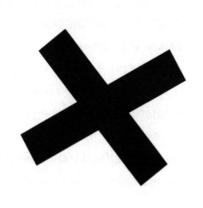

EDITOR'S PREFACE

Even a few months ago, when the Squint series
editors decided we wanted a book on Donald
Trump – clearly an icon of the age we live in – it
was possible to see him as a mostly amusing
sideshow. One could get lofty and compare him
to Charles Foster Kane (another ambiguous rich
man fighting from the podium for the little guy),
or P.T. Barnum, who once said a sucker was born
every minute, and sold circuses to America. Soon,
though, more vociferous critics began to note his
mannerisms becoming more Italianate, circa Il
Duce. More recently still, darker comparisons were
made between his pledge rallies and Nazi events.
As Trump has risen – spectacularly and in full view
of an amazed world – to become the most feared,
compelling and eccentric American politician in
living memory, so too have the stakes. So this book
darkened as well, in the process.

   Oliver Jones started to write this book as
a sort of study-guide to the many faces of Trump
– his memes, his phraseology, his rhetoric – a
field-guide to the florid, over the top and at times
outrageous pronouncements, insults, and innuendo
that seem to issue forth from the billionaire daily.
Always shocking, sometimes funny, Trump was not

expected to get this far without more of a fight – but his fellow candidates were either too worthy, too eloquent, too intelligent, or too weak to really knock him back. Trump, the pugilist, has moved relentlessly on, becoming less the comic reality-TV host and hotelier with curiously coiffed hair and more the man from Stephen King's *The Dead Zone* – the terrifying President who just may push the nuclear button.

This is a book with much insight into what Trump has said these past ten months, as he has overcome all obstacles and debating rivals to master a new kind of media communication – one that transcends the media, defies opinion and short-circuits the ability of the media to defend themselves from his charismatic, bizarre performances. He has become grist for the mill, often the biggest story of the day, breaking news and news that stays news, in Pound's phrase – apposite because Trump has created a sort of poetic approach to politics. He is all symbol, all assertion, all fantastical hyperbole – an anti-Whitman. One *Guardian* columnist called him an anti-Christ, and even the Pope seemed to condemn some of his beliefs as being non-Christian.

Generals, CIA guys, former presidents, think-tanks, all warn that Trump is bad news.

Jones has given us, finally, an anatomy of a masquerade so brilliant and complex it has dazzled the American voters who flock to hear him, and rush to vote for him – for Trump is not one person. He contains multitudes and his sub-divided character represents the sub-divisions of an army of me. Trump's secret weapon is he plays a number of major American stereotypical roles very well – maybe as well or better than Reagan did. I found this book informative, amusing, frightening, and very readable. I hope you will too. It should be read by everyone who is concerned about what comes next, for America, for Trump, and for the rest of the world. Is this the trump of doom?

Dr Todd Swift
Director of Eyewear Publishing Ltd

London, UK
3 April, 2016

THE TRUMP TIMELINE

2015

June 16th – Trump announces his presidential bid during which he claims Mexican immigrants are killers and rapists and he will build a wall between the USA and Mexico.

June 23rd – Trump launches the first of his many attacks on Jeb Bush, declaring *"I can't believe Bush is in first place. This guy can't negotiate his way out of a paper bag. So I'm in second place to Bush? I hate it!"*

June 28th – Trump defends his comments about Mexicans, observing *"I'm talking about people that are from all over that are killers and rapists and they're coming into this country."*

July 8th – Trump goes after Clinton. *"Hillary Clinton was the worst Secretary of State in the history of the United States."*

July 11th – the first major rally of Trump's campaign occurs in Phoenix, Arizona.

July 18th – Trump goes after Senator John McCain

at the Family Leadership Summit. *"He's not a war hero. He was a war hero because he was captured. I like people who weren't captured."*

July 21st – then former governor of Texas Rick Perry. *"He put on glasses so people think he's smart. People can see through the glasses."*

August 6th – first GOP debate. Trump is the early frontrunner at 23.4%, followed by Jeb Bush. Trump is grilled by Fox News anchor Megyn Kelly over offensive remarks about women, including referring to them as "fat pigs, dogs, slobs, and disgusting animals."

August 7th –Trump suggests Kelly was on her period at the time. *"You could see there was blood coming out of her eyes. Blood coming out of her wherever."*

August 11th –Trump criticises Bernie Sanders for listening to representatives of Black Lives Matter at a rally. *"I thought that was disgusting. That showed such weakness, the way he was taken away by two young women. That will never happen with me. I don't know if I'll do the fighting myself, or if other people will, but that was a disgrace."*

September 9th – in a *Rolling Stone* profile, Trump outrages with comments on fellow candidate Carly Fiona *"Look at that face! Would anyone vote for that? Can you imagine that, the face of our next president?"*

September 16th – second GOP debate, where a strong performance by Marco Rubio sees him pull ahead. Final debate featuring Scott Walker, who drops out soon after. Trump still leads with 24%.

September 17th – Trump approves of a rallyer claiming that President Obama is a Muslim and that Muslims are a problem.

September 23rd – Trump goes after Hillary Clinton *"Do you know the word 'shrill'? She can be kind of shrill (funny voice)"* and Chris Christie. *"That room was hot. I mean, poor Chris Christie!"*

October 4th – on ABC's *This Week*, Trump claims there is nothing the government can do to stop mass shootings, saying of shooters *"They can be sick as hell and they're geniuses in a certain way"*.

October 10th – Trump falsely accuses John Kasich of being on the board of Lehman Brothers during the financial crisis.

October 28th – third GOP debate. Trump's polls at 20.2%, closely followed by Ben Carson at 19.8 %. They force the debate to be limited to two hours.

November 2nd –Trump begins his characterisation of Marco Rubio as *"the one that sweats the most. He's the youngest but I have never seen any human being sweat like that."*

November 10th – fourth GOP debate. Trump and Carson nearly tied at 24.8 and 24.4 percent respectively.

November 12th – compares Ben Carson to a child molester *"It's in the book that he's got a pathological temper. That's a big problem because you don't cure that. As an example: child molesting. You don't cure these people."*

November 13th – ISIS mass shootings in Paris lead to a rise in popularity for candidates seen as being tough on immigration, such as Trump and Cruz. Carson, by contrast, steadily loses support from here on, and is replaced by Cruz as Trump's main rival.

Novermber 19th – Trump tells NBC that all American Muslims should be registered in a database.

November 25th – Trump seemingly mocks a disabled New York Times reporter by flailing his hands about, and making odd facial grimaces.

December 7th – Trump proposes banning all Muslims from entering the USA. *"Donald J Trump is calling for a total and complete shutdown of Muslims entering the United States until our country's representatives can figure out what the hell is going on."*

December 15th – fifth GOP debate. Trump pulls ahead of Carson with 27.7% to 27.6%.

December 21st – Trump informs a Michigan rally that Clinton got "schlonged" by Obama in their 2008 contest for the Democratic nomination.

2016

January 8th – a Muslim woman is ejected from a Trump rally in South Carolina. *"There is hatred against us that is unbelievable. It's their hatred, it's not our hatred,"* says Trump.

January 14th – sixth GOP debate. Trump increases his lead to 35.8%.

January 20th – Trump's devastating remark that Jeb Bush is "low energy". Sarah Palin endorses Trump.

January 28th – seventh GOP debate. Trump boycotts the debate due to prior confrontations with Megyn Kelly.

February 1st – Cruz narrowly beats Trump and Rubio to take Iowa, becoming the first Hispanic person to win a presidential caucus. Rubio enjoys a brief moment as the probable establishment candidate.

February 6th – eighth GOP debate. A comedy of errors during the introduction of candidates. Under attack from Chris Christie, Rubio repeats the same rehearsed line five times in his worst performance of the campaign.

February 8th – Trump echoes a rallyer calling Ted Cruz "a pussy".

February 9th – Trump takes New Hampshire.

February 13th – ninth GOP debate. Trump calls the Iraq war "a big, fat mistake".

February 18th – Trump claims that Pope Francis is the pawn in an anti-Trump conspiracy by the Mexican government.

February 20th – Trump takes South Carolina. Jeb Bush suspends his campaign, but not before having infamously bought a gun engraved with his name, and then tweeted about it.

February 23rd – Trump takes Nevada.

February 25th – tenth GOP debate. Rubio and Cruz join forces to attack Trump, criticising his business acumen, his lying, his use of illegal labour.

February 27th – Chris Christie endorses Trump.

February 28th – Trump fails to condemn former KKK grand wizard and Trump endorser David Duke, saying *"I don't even know anything about what you're talking about with white supremacy or white supremacists."* He later blames a faulty earpiece for the omission.

March 1st – Super Tuesday. Trump emerges as the likely nominee, taking Alabama, Arkansas, Georgia, Massachusetts, Tennessee, Vermont and Virginia. Cruz takes Alaska, Oklahoma and Texas, Rubio takes Minnesota. On the Democrat side, Hillary emerges as the likely Democrat nominee, though Bernie Sanders marches on.

March 3rd – Mitt Romney speaks out against Trump, calling him a "fraud" and advising tactical voting against him. Eleventh GOP debate. Trump insists there is "no problem" with the size of his genitalia in response to Rubio's "small hands" jibe.

March 4th – Ben Carson suspends his campaign.

March 5th – Cruz takes Kansas and Maine. Trump takes Kentucky and Louisiana.

March 8th – Trump takes Michigan, Mississippi and Hawaii. Cruz takes Idaho.

March 10th – twelfth GOP debate.

March 11th – Trump cancels rally at University of Illinois in Chicago after the protestors storm the event. Ben Carson endorses Trump.

March 15th - "Super Tuesday II". Trump takes Illinois, Missouri, North Carolina and North Mariana Islands. Rubio loses Florida, his home state, to Trump. Kasich takes his home state, Ohio.

March 16th - Marco Rubio suspends his campaign.

March 21st - last GOP debate is cancelled after Trump and Kasich withdraw from the event.

March 22nd - Trump takes Arizona. Cruz wins Utah.

March 23rd - Jeb Bush endorses Cruz.

DRAMATIS PERSONAE

THE REPUBLICANS

Donald TRUMP:
Protagonist of the Trump campaign. A billionaire, celebrity and businessman who throws his hat in the political ring, gaining widespread popular support through incendiary, sometimes off-colour speech-acts. He is funny, rude, hot-tempered, and seemingly full of self-regard. Increasingly he evokes memories of the 1930s in his rallies, and often speaks in front of his giant plane emblazoned with the word TRUMP.

Ted CRUZ:
Trump's main challenger for the Republican nomination. A Texas senator, lawyer and Tea Party candidate who is considered the most abrasive, anti-establishment, populist candidate until Trump appears on the scene. Cruz becomes the moderate alternative to Trump and the GOP's champion after Trump takes the lead in the Republican race. A popular meme (falsely) suggests he may be The Zodiac Killer. He is a brilliant debater. He becomes accused of multiple affairs by some journalists.

Marco RUBIO:

A Florida senator, attorney and candidate for the Republican nomination. Youthful, handsome, golden-tongued and politically gifted, he is nevertheless side-lined in the race. Beginning his campaign with intelligent optimism, he is later drawn into aping Trump's coarse language, making comments about Trump's wet pants and hand size. He is subsequently shown regretting this course of action. There are rumours of homosocial foam parties in his student days.

Jeb BUSH:

Son of former president George H. W. Bush, brother of former president George W. Bush and at one-time leading candidate for the Republican nomination. "Bush was on the wrong side of the most galvanising issues for voters, he himself was a maladroit campaigner and his campaign was riven by internal disagreements and a crippling fear that left them paralyzed and unable to react to Trump"[0]. Bush drops out of the race shortly after tweeting a picture of his gun with the caption "America." He may best be remembered as the man who pathetically asked an audience to clap for him.

Ben CARSON:

One of America's most popular people. A brilliant African-American brain surgeon who pioneered procedures to separate cranially-conjoined twins. Unfortunately, he comes across as a bit of a joke on the debate stage. A soft-spoken, other-worldly thinker of bizarre and often unexpected ideas, his own memoir confesses to childhood rages with hammers. He ends his once-promising run for the candidacy in a whimper of glory, unexpectedly endorsing Trump.

Chris CHRISTIE:

The 55th Governor of New Jersey and candidate for the Republican nomination. Known prior to the campaign as a heavy-set, straight-talking everyman, after his poor campaign performance and endorsement of Trump he faces an intense media backlash, ridicule and calls for his resignation as governor.

Sarah PALIN:

Former governor of Alaska catapulted to tabloid fame as Senator John McCain's running mate in his doomed 2008 presidential campaign, during which her celebrity quickly eclipsed his. A figure in equal parts admired, ridiculed and fantasised over in the popular imagination. A powerful figure in grassroots conservatism, she aided the rise of both Ted Cruz and Donald Trump, endorsing Cruz in 2012, but favouring Trump in 2016.

The other candidates: John KASICH, Rand PAUL, Mike HUCKABEE, Carly FIONA, Rick SANTORUM and Jim GILMORE. They enjoy varying levels of success.

THE DEMOCRATS

Barack OBAMA:
President of the United States of America and the
first African-American president in its history.
Winner of the Nobel Peace Prize and popular
overseas, domestically he faces criticism over
his attempts to reduce foreign interventionism
and introduce a form of socialised medicine with
Obamacare. He is haunted by failed promises, but
retains a sense of dignity, decency and courage.

Hillary CLINTON:
The former United States Secretary of State,
former First Lady (married to Bill Clinton) and
Democratic frontrunner for the 2016 nomination.
Policy-orientated and pragmatic, she is the
establishment antithesis to Trump and aims to be
the first female president of the United States.
Once popular as a meme in her shades, she has
now been somewhat eclipsed in public affections
by....

Bernie SANDERS:
Vermont senator and candidate for the Democratic
nomination, Sanders has become the leading
progressive voice in America on almost every major

policy issue. The unexpected main rival to Clinton for the nomination, Sanders draws huge crowds, is popular online and among the young, and polls highly, but has so far been unable to close the gap in delegates. Bespectacled, Jewish, cantankerous, his grumpy manner cuts through all the BS and rationally explicates a passionately socialist position. Sometimes called the American Jeremy Corbyn.

On our televisions and in our unconscious, the image: Donald Trump, sitting in a dozen interview chairs, standing at a dozen different podiums, blasting a dozen press microphones with all the potency his mouth can muster. Donald Trump, lopsided grin creasing his tanned face into a thousand folds. Donald Trump, whose raised, innocent eyebrows cause international outrage on a biweekly basis.

This is not a book about Donald Trump. That is to say, it is not about the New York billionaire, raised in Queens and graduated from New York Military Academy. This is not about the shrewd businessman who authored a number of self-help bestsellers including *The Art of the Deal* and *Time To Get Tough, Making America #1 Again*. It is not even about the hopeful who unexpectedly chose to stand for the Republican nomination against all odds and advice on June 16th of 2015.

This is a book about the wholly separate figure that has emerged in the intervening period, during which the Trump campaign has transformed from a rude joke into the most divisive and discussed phenomenon in contemporary politics. This is about the Trump phenomenon: an elongated mass narrative, caricature of a successful American and revelation about our culture. This is about how Trump replaced the political virtues of Aristotle, Plato and the founding fathers – sagacity and wisdom – with the virtues of the action movie hero: masculine indifference, anti-intellectualism, 'guts' and a steady source of one-line put-downs. This is about the figure who, in so doing, cast the entire American political process in the mould of a Hollywood movie – a down-to-earth protagonist's sweaty struggle against snobbish aristocrats, a carbine-rifle-and-grenade assault on the complex systems that distort the simple truth of good against evil. This is a book about how Trump made a foil of the American political establishment.

This is also not especially a book criticising Trump. As we shall see, Trump is immune to criticism – particularly when it comes from what might be called the liberal intelligentsia – and has benefitted from every one of the many attacks made on him. Correspondingly, I don't feel obliged to attack, undermine or otherwise mount an agenda against Trump. The Trump story as I narrate it is not intended to express facts or change minds, but to show how easy it is to weave a grand narrative around a figure, and how dangerous.

This is not a book about Trump because we no longer have access to the 'real' Trump. There is no politician called Donald Trump lying behind Trump's media image, no agent of reform or representative of the people. Trump's indifference to politics renders him invulnerable to political literature and invisible to us. It also makes him the perfect vehicle for forces bigger than himself. This is a book about the media presentation of Trump and our response to it. This is a book about how the media created a Trump for us to respond to. The Trump we can access exists only as a series of vignettes, or faces, and these are what I shall present.

FACES OF TRUMP

My thesis is that the Trump phenomenon is
a confluence of American linguistic clichés
and adversarial, theatrical relations between
politicians, permitted by the frame-by-frame
dependency of the campaign narrative on simple
images and rounded poll percentages. This is the
Trump that is revealed to us through television
and the internet: a collection of soundbites, jibes
and grimaces. The figure that emerges forms a
collection of characters that I have assembled into
the following sixteen 'Faces of Trump'.

TRUMP THE MAN

> TRUMP: Somebody said to me the other day, a reporter, a very nice reporter, 'But, Mr. Trump, you're not a nice person.'

> AUDIENCE MEMBER: We don't need nice.

Our subject is a stocky 6'2" man in his late middle age. In the public eye he is normally seen wearing Brioni suits and a trademark 'double combover'. His eyes are an alarming blue. He became our subject during a speech on June 16th of 2015, when he announced he would run for president in 2016. For our purposes, June 16th is the 'Trump' birthday, the moment his character traits ceased to belong to him as an individual and became propositions about the country he has begun to transform.

It all too easy to disparage Trump, living at the top of his tower in a Louis XIV-style triplex, with his much-ridiculed hair, his professed mania for making money, the clan of Trumps in his employ and the buildings he names after himself. It is easy to vilify him, and unnecessary. Trump has made it into prominence by playing the antichrist to every liberal agenda. He has so successfully provoked every area of the left-leaning press and every blogger and commentator with a shred of conscience that he has made himself into the primary figure in opposition to liberal, culturally relativistic values.

Thus, he has become a rallying point for every force in America seeking to dislodge the relative sanity and sanguinity of the Obama administration. However, among Trump's many targets, the most important is not Mexico, China, ISIS, Islam, or even 'the establishment'. It is the media, because it is by attacking the media that he became immune to its attacks and able to court media attention with no repercussions.

This has allowed him to seize control of the election cycle by using media coverage to boost his poll numbers – which in turn increases his media coverage in a self-reinforcing pattern. Paradoxically, to demonise Trump is to give him strength. As a political image, he is the hydra to Obama's Apollo, drawing strength from all the criticism and outrage directed at him. The demonization of Trump is a tool for him to seize control of the dialogue and appear as a rebel, defiant of a prudish liberal press.

So we will not demonise Trump. Trump is not a bloodthirsty fanatic out to destroy liberal values – he is a businessman and celebrity making the coup of his life. He is not a scheming politician skilfully balancing fashionable hatreds – he is a fame-hungry consumer being led in a media dance that is itself powerless to control its appetite for increased viewership. Though Trump says racist and militaristic things, most likely he is not a racist, or a hawk, except through passive consumption of those ideas. Trump is not an ideologue, he is the opposite: a man who follows the ideas that have been suggested to him by our communal zeitgeist.

TRUMP THE FAMILY

> TRUMP: That's true. But actually I am. I
> think I am a nice person. People that know
> me, like me. Does my family like me? I think
> so, right. Look at my family. I'm proud of my
> family.

> (APPLAUSE)

Trump often brags about his wealth, but never
about his wealthy origins. His mother is Mary Anne,
a Scot who immigrates into the United States in
the 1930s. There she meets and marries Fred Trump,
the son of German immigrants[1]. Fred is a 'tough,
strong businessman'[2] and a successful real estate
developer in Queens and Brooklyn. Mary gives birth
to baby Trump in Queens, New York, fourth of five
children. In stark contrast to his son, Fred Trump is
reserved and thrifty, though in true Trumpian form
he does buy a blue Cadillac with his initials on the
license plate.

At the time of his death in 1999, he is
worth between 250 and 300 million dollars. He is
investigated in 1954 for profiteering from public
contracts and subsequently subject of a lawsuit by
his tenants. Woody Guthrie mentions Fred Trump

in a song he writes while staying in a Trump Beach Haven apartment, suggesting that 'Old Man Trump' is stirring up and profiteering from racial hatred by discriminating against black tenants. In 1973 the US Justice Department files a suit against the Trump organisation for refusing to rent to African Americans.

The Trump siblings grow up in a secluded, suburban part of an otherwise ethnically diverse Queens in a complex which, with its Greek columns, eerily echoes the White House. According to Trump's biographer, Michael D'Antonio, they are raised to be competitive, beholden to the Fred Trump mantra 'you're a killer; you're a king'[3]. D'Antonio claims that Donald gets into trouble at school for violence, injuring teachers and students. Unable to control the rampaging 11-year-old (just as we are unable to control him now) his parents send him to the New York Military Academy. After graduating, he joins the family firm. There is a tradition of 'self-made men' in the family[4], though as heir to an enormous fortune young Donald is anything but that. When Trump moves to Manhattan, he's 29. Though it takes him until the age of 29 to fly the nest, he is characterised as fearless and bold – even by me.

Matt Frei, in his Channel 4 documentary *The Mad World of Donald Trump* argues that the mob domination of 1970s Manhattan real estate and the accompanying attitude shaped Donald's view of the world, drawing on the following quote:

> TRUMP: I look on people as being in many cases very vicious and, unless you're gonna have a certain way [sic], you're gonna be eaten alive, especially in New York City.

Trump redevelops run-down buildings, such as the Commodore hotel. Here is where pro-Trump accounts begin to turn towards deliberate myth. Trump talks his way into the contract through 'sheer force of will'[5] and obtains an enormous bank loan. Right here is the start of Trump as he would like to be known: the plucky, sandy-haired Donald making it off the street and into ownership of a derelict hotel, which he covers in reflective glass. The physics of the story seem to suggest that Trump knows the hidden infrastructure that connects the man on the street to the interior of Trump's glossy hotels, but in practise he had every advantage it is possible to have.

The Trump buildings, like the Trump character, benefit from being gross, overweight and overly ostentatious. They are baubles dangled before the proletariat, testaments to the glory of Trump. And Trump Tower is the setting for the first stop on our Trump journey, his announcement on June 16th of 2015 that he would run for president.

Analysis of Trump's 2016 announcement
TRUMP: It's great to be at Trump Tower (jumps straight in with the Trump brand) and it's an honour to have everybody here, this is beyond anybody's expectations (anecdotal evidence of the general superlative quality of everything he is involved in), there's been no crowd like this ... I can tell you some of the candidates they went in, they didn't know the air conditioner didn't work, they sweated like dogs (same technique, this time proving the idiocy and incompetence of the opposition. Also makes them into animals) they didn't know the room was too big (one of Trump's favourite words) because they didn't have anybody there (illogical, Trump's version of being smart or ironic is to say things that don't make sense as if they do). How are they gonna beat ISIS? (Rather neatly brings in the argument that Trump's excessive competence is necessary in the terrifying age we live in). I don't think it's gonna happen (flatly expresses an opinion. His supporters love it when he does this. It's like a

generalised catchphrase). Our country is in serious trouble (an all-purpose statement which will find easy agreement and which is impossible to analyse or disprove. Generality is like Trump's superpower; it grants him invulnerability to logic, fact and argument). We don't have victories any more. (Harkens back to an ideal age of conquest and moral simplicity. A popular tactic of which Trump is the world's second most effective proponent, after radical Islam). We used to have victories, but we don't have 'em. When was the last time anybody saw us beating (readies for a violent combo of inverse-anecdotal sucker-punches. It's not often that a theoretical eyewitness is called upon to identify an abstract event which s/he did not see), let's say, CHINA (his grandiose posture is of being able to personally take on China) in a trade deal?

They kill us (uses military rhetoric for emphasis). I beat China all the time (draws an equivalence between Trump's trade deals with individual Chinese corporations and the international relationship between China and the USA. This is another popular political tactic: inviting us to imagine the whole government can be just like a private citizen. It is most prominently used by austerity governments inaccurately comparing government finance to household

finance, cue slogan: 'spending within our means').
When did we beat Japan? At anything? They send
their cars over by the millions (treats nations
as individual agents, linked to previous point.
Labelling diverse groups as single entities will be
a key Trumpian tactic, and the 'millions of cars'
prep the audience for similarly catastrophic claims
regarding immigration). When was the last time you
saw a Chevrolet in Tokyo? (a good phrase, hats off).
It doesn't exist, folks. They beat us all the time.

When do we beat Mexico at the border?
(rhetorically unites America's competitive
disadvantages economically with its immigration
tensions. Ironically, immigration from Mexico
makes American business more, not less,
competitive, due to lower wages.) They're laughing
us, at our stupidity (characterises foreign nations
as contemptuous and Americaphobic. Also cashes
in on lingering resentment at the worldwide
ridicule of last Republican president, George W.
Bush, for his perceived stupidity) and now they are
beating us economically (this isn't true[6]), they are
not our friend, believe me. But they're killing us
economically. (Trump normally reverses his and's
and but's. This gives the impression, when he is
making a caveat, that he is reinforcing a point). The
US has become the dumping ground for everybody

else's problems (one of those unverifiable Trump statements. It also plays into a myth of strong, American individualism: America as John Wayne with lesser nations as parasitic. Blames domestic unease on foreign nations. If it seems paradoxical that Trump blames other nations for America's problems, while advocating greater intervention in foreign nations, that's because it is. It is nice to think that perhaps paradox powers revolution and that the elemental force that flips an impossible proposition between true and false could spin the gears of change on its way.) It's true. And these are the best and the finest.

When Mexico sends its people, they're not sending their best, they're not sending you, they're not sending YOU (emphasises the otherness of other nationals). They're sending people who have lots of problems. And they're bringing their problems with us (a grammatical error, but an accidental truth: US consumption – its drug problem – is the main source of funds for the Mexican narcotic industry[7]). They're bringing drugs, they're rapists, and some, I assume, are good people (another switch of 'and' and 'but' to annul a qualifier. This particular quote gained considerable notoriety and will be explored more fully in a later chapter). But I speak to border guards (unlikely and anecdotal) and they tell us (switch of 'I' to 'us' attempts to render anecdote as general truth) what we're getting. And it only makes common sense (uses the flexible notion of 'common sense' against every other kind of sense, such as economic or logical). It only makes common sense. They're sending us not the right people. It's coming from more than Mexico, (uses an indefinite 'it'. The ambiguity allows the listener to substitute her own experience of the vague catastrophe Trump hints at but never defines – a poet's technique). It's coming probably, probably, from the Middle East (uses 'probably' to suggest some kind of reasonable balance of evidence, particularly when he has none). But we don't know because we have no protection and we have no competence (delegates his own ignorance to the opposition).

Contrast: an Obama 2008 announcement in which Obama offers a carefully argued life narrative that justifies his run at the presidency. He is inclusive, compassionate and reasonable: 'it is here we learned to disagree without being disagreeable'[8]. He is a spiritual ambassador for ancient values, with Renaissance phrases such as 'liberty and equality depend on the active participation of an awakened electorate'[9]. Obama asks us to listen to each other and assume the best in people instead of the worst. He also gives specific examples of his accomplishments. Looking back on it, Obama comes across as a master in outdated sincerity and political technique.

Trump offers no experience, no friendly hand and no argument. Trump knows America is too old and bitter for compassion. Obama speaks of 'the essential decency of the American people'. Trump speaks of America as 'the world's dumping ground'. Yet Trump is seen as patriotic and Obama as internationalist. Trump's victory would be a tragic refutation of everything Obama tried to change in America.

Contrast: 'Humbled' Trump

Andrew Rosenthal: *At around 2:30 on Monday afternoon, at a rally in Cedar Rapids, Iowa, Donald Trump was loudly, confidently and repeatedly proclaiming his impending victory in Iowa. Just before 10 pm, he was acting like he had never expected to win, and like coming in second was a huge accomplishment.*[10]

TRUMP: On June 16th when we started this journey, there were seventeen candidates. I was told by everybody (an uncertain general statement

masked as an anecdote) do not go to Iowa you
could never finish even in the top ten (retroactively
revises expectations massively downward) and I
said I have friends in Iowa I know a lot of people
in Iowa (simplifies the electoral process to a high
school popularity contest) I think they're really
like me, let's give it a shot (sudden indifference to
winning – high contrast to his previous 'winning
is all that matters' approach) they said 'don't
do it' I said 'I had to do it' (frames his failure as
brave rebellion) and we finished second and I
wanna tell you something. I'm just honoured, really
honoured and I wanna congratulate Ted, and I
wanna congratulate all of the incredible candidates
including Mike Huckabee who's become a really
good friend of mine so congratulations, everybody,
congratulations...

While Trump's first emotional port of call is always
contempt and rage, in defeat he finds plenty of
refuge in happiness and contentment. There is
a shift to 'We' and emphasis on his family as
together in the fight. These are not-so-subtle
ways of shifting the onus of failure onto shoulders
other than his own – since his campaign is built
on a facade of untainted personal success. One
doubts he is embarrassed at the abrupt volte-face.

Rosenthal also observes: 'It's impossible to know whether Mr. Trump understands that his slack campaign organization in Iowa may have cost him dearly here. Kenneth P. Vogel of Politico said Mr. Trump spent almost as much on hats as he did on payroll.'

Compare: 'Magnanimous' Trump

Maggie Haberman: *With Super Tuesday behind him, Mr. Trump was looking ahead to the general election at a news conference at his Mar-a-Lago property in Florida. The candidate, best known for scathing insults and divisive language, made his best attempt at magnanimity. 'Believe me, I'm a unifier,' Mr. Trump said.* [11]

TRUMP: Thanks very much, I appreciate that. This has been an amazing evening, we already won five major states and it looks like we could win six or seven or eight or nine. It's really good. I wanna congratulate Ted on the winning of Texas. He worked hard on it and I know how hard he worked actually so I congratulate Ted Cruz on that win, that was an excellent win. (This opens the brief window when Rubio, not Cruz, appeared to be the stop-Trump candidate, hence a rare instance of condescending collegiality) Uh, We're gonna make

America great again folks, we're going to make it great again. And, you know, I watched Hillary's speech (shifting up a gear to set up Hillary vs Trump as the projected outcome) and she's talking about wages have been poor and everything's poor and everything's doing badly, but we're going to make it – she's been there for so long. I mean, if she hasn't straightened it out by now, she's not going to straighten it out in the next four years (colloquial argument). It's just going to become worse and worse (brandishing the fear of failure at the whole electorate). She wants to make America whole again and I'm trying to figure out what is that all about. Make America great again is going to be much better than making America whole again (a sharp encapsulation of Trump's individualistic ethics).

By the time Super Tuesday rolls around, Trump has successfully transformed the campaign narrative into one of Everybody vs. Trump, with widespread calls for the Republican party to consolidate in opposition. Even the Democratic nomination has become a question of whether Bernie or Hillary is more likely to beat Trump in the general election (rather than the relative merits of their campaign platforms).

TRUMP THE ANTI-OBAMA

TRUMP: And it's going to get worse, because remember, Obamacare really kicks in in '16, 2016. Obama is going to be out playing golf. He might be on one of my courses. I would invite him, I actually would say. I have the best courses in the world, so I'd say, you what, if he wants to – I have one right next to the White House, right on the Potomac. If he'd like to play, that's fine.

(APPLAUSE)

TRUMP: In fact, I'd love him to leave early and play, that would be a very good thing.

(LAUGHTER)

Trump begins his political career disparaging Barack Obama and in many ways his entire candidacy can be seen as a reaction to or negative shadow of Obama's extremely competent politics. In an eerie preview of the knack for controversy he would soon display, Trump used talk shows to call for Obama to show his birth certificate in 2011, a move that seemingly served no purpose other than to give Trump some media space. He succeeded, however, in forcing the President to release his birth certificate, while publically mocking Trump – little imagining the power similarly absurd claims would come to posses in Trump's mouth.

Aside: Obama Roasts Trump

> Trump sits stock still, the camera catching him in profile, hair forming a sickle among the glitterati, neck a grey formless mass with the back of his head. Obama humorously presents 'The Trump White House', a garish mock-up of a Trump casino-style White House with Trump's name glitzed on the front – not so funny now.

Trump is also a sharp contrast to Obama's successors-to-be, Hillary Clinton and Bernie Sanders.

What Trump has in common with Obama, at least in terms of his election campaign, is that he has created a dividing line between himself and other candidates. Obama was very successful in making a vote for Obama symbolise a vote for 'Hope', a change in the way the country is governed, the start of compassionate government and so on. Apart from his admirable personal qualities, it was his potential as first Black President of the United States that lent credence to that mythology. Trump has also been very proficient at creating dividing lines, though in his case by appealing to the precise opposite – a xenophobic zeal in advocating for narrowly defined American interests, symbolised in the current campaign by his willingness to offend and insult and his promises to expel and beat down. This means he is the first candidate since Obama to give voters the sense that a vote for Trump is a significant choice – hence the fear he instils in liberal voters and the sense of positive choice and empowerment he instils in his supporters – a sense that is normally lacking at election time.

With Trump as presumptive Republican nominee, this world vs Trump storyline becomes increasingly pronounced. Celebrities, government officials and figures from the history of the Republican Party weigh in, one after the other, to denounce Trump. Editors and late-night comedians form something of an informal stop-Trump bloc, likening him to 'authoritarians and xenophobes', 'America's Ahmedinejad', 'Hitler' and 'cancer'[12].

The Hitler comparison is later echoed by Mexican President Peña Nieto, Anne Frank's stepsister and the former governor of New Jersey, among others, and is one of the few times

Trump has been forced on the defensive. From the Republican side, ex-presidential candidates Mitt Romney and John McCain, former New York mayor Michael Bloomberg, former CIA director Michael Hayde and the anti-Trump open letter by 65 GOP 'national security experts', coalesce around the contention that Trump would be a danger to national security as president. They put that danger down to inexperience, idiocy or malevolence, but the real reason is the one many commentators have already spotted.

It is Trump's compulsion to seek attention. Trump's offensive statements and extreme policies are too often seen as wild schemes of a genuine bigot or Machiavellian ploys of a master manipulator. The truth is they are attention-seeking acts that any of us could have come up with, but whose effect on Trump's campaign has been so great that they now act as a blueprint for contemporary right-wing populism.

Trump is seen as a manipulator of media, but actually he is more susceptible to popular opinion than most. Hence his childish personal letters to people who have insulted or rejected him[13], hence the sacrifice of his own businesses in pursuit of conspicuous investment and hence his consistency in doubling down every time a bluff is called. The danger is that Trump, a specimen who is more, not less, carried away by his media presentation than his supporters, is being taught to play the role of shameless provocateur (an act whose ropes he learned on the celebrity circuit) and as a result there are no brakes on what he can be compelled to do to please his supporters or respond to criticism. The recklessness that gives him strength as a candidate makes him unhinged as a leader. And when even the most reserved and respectful of presidents are constantly baited and ridiculed, we can only imagine the drastic lengths to which Trump would go, protecting an impossible self-image with all the immense power of the United States at his disposal.

TRUMP THE ADVERT

> AUDIENCE: We want Trump. We want Trump. We want Trump. We want Trump.

> TRUMP: Well, you need somebody.

Politics always presents us with a star-studded, Hollywood cast. Even unassuming politicians will have some glamorous nuance teased out of them: buck-toothed Clinton, leering at the camera; hapless Bush stumbling over some choice phrase; lanky Obama's ironic shrug. Now we have 'The Donald', slouching his way to glory in a triumph of expedient outrage. Politics reduces all its players to caricatures and no-one benefits from this as much as Trump, a man devastatingly simple to begin with and hence a man who translates exceptionally well at election time.

But Trump also reveals the threat to politics that this theatre represents. He reveals that American politics has adapted badly to new communications and that while individual politicians have learnt to play characters, the campaign system as a whole is dependent on the use of donations to ubiquitously disseminate images of the candidate. Trump, with his riches and independent celebrity, is not attached to the political establishment by the same umbilical cord.

Politics is in many ways still catching up to the modern world. Parallel to the demonization of the public sector relative to the private sector (as a cumbersome bureaucracy) is the strange anachronism that politics has yet to explicitly embrace itself as a form of advertising. This is in spite of the very obvious attempts to irrationally link a candidate with the values of his electorate, whether that be Trump and aspiration or Obama and tolerance.

Just as it pays dividends in business to link your product with a value – smoking with independence, cars with power, perfume with desirability[14] – so does it pay to link your politician with a value. In the case of Trump, that value is success. I don't consider this a particularly controversial statement: that campaign politics, at least, is advertising.

If politics is advertising then the electoral campaign is a process of gradual hypnosis. Simply giving citizens information and expecting informed decisions is a technique obsolete in American PR since at least the 1920s. What's astonishing is that it's still not the norm for politicians to speak about this – that there remains the myth of reasonable debate, fact-based policy and the autonomous will of the electorate. The only place this idea seems to survive is in artificial debates between politicians. Trump does not go so far as to make explicit what everybody knows, but he certainly does not condescend to use facts or reason.

Politics of emotion stands in contrast to political appeals to function and necessity. Politicians say that a policy is needed, or will help people. This is a moralistic hang-up that advertising outgrew a long time ago. No advert seeks to prove to you that smoking will make you more popular, a car will make you more confident, or a brand of perfume will make you more desirable. Instead, these things are implied through images and slogans that make no claim to fact or truth, but simply stand as they are, implying what they do. Fundamental desires can be recalibrated by images to induce purchases.

Man's desires overshadow his needs in an affluent society. This is why America is susceptible to the politician it wants, rather than the one it needs. Trump is a big step in this direction because he has abandoned fact in favour of unashamed fiction. But even he relies on the clone crutches of fear and hate and has not (or cannot) explore the more profitable avenues of sex appeal and fashion.

Appealing to negative, life-and-death issues in a society which does not face death – except as a paranoid fantasy – is a holdover from less promising times. That fear issues can still be used to win elections is a sign either of politics being old fashioned, or that all the more positive motivators – such as sex and wealth – have been saturated by private businesses, leaving politicians to fight over terror and poverty. What happens when successive generations of politicians, business owners and PR elites operate on a mass society to engineer consent, shaping opinion and attitudes in their own interest – and then future ranks of ad-makers are drawn from that society? You get a reflexive feedback loop that ceases to be self-aware. Hence Donald Trump, product of a recursive system with no self-control: a man who believes his own propaganda.

A specific anachronism we should draw our attention to is the system of feedback during campaigns – the opinion polls. These still use a deliberately neutral language. They seems to assume rationality and that, given a neutral question, the real will of the people can be divined. But it is impossible to interpret a coherent voice of the people – it is too frequent and tends in no direction except that of increasing outrage. The totality of the electorate's opinion is too diverse to be expressed by a politician. The authentic voice of the American people is silent, because its contradictions cannot be expressed by a politician as the solution to its problems. Instead we have opinion polls, which are just as much a part of what influences the electorate as an expression of electoral opinion.

It is statistical fact that the candidate with the greatest media coverage normally has the best poll results[15]. Media coverage is a much better predictor of poll results than favourability ratings (for which Trump has the highest 'unfavourable' rating of any candidate, followed by Clinton). This creates a self-reinforcing loop, as a candidate with better poll results gets more media coverage. Trump has hacked this system very efficiently by attacking the media and getting more coverage as a result – negative coverage, to be sure – and then striking back at that negative coverage in return for even more of it. In spite of what I have said about Trump linking himself with values like success and 'winning', more important is his domination of the communal dialogue, which is the combustion engine that powers Donald Trump's campaign.

But Trump, as I envisage him, is not conscious of the clever game he is playing.

His shield against speaking an overly political language that the electorate do not understand is to be illiterate in that language. He is simply doing his best to win elections by saying what he is expected to say. His mechanism of divining what that is is that of the class clown, seeking maximum provocation and disruption. If all of America is Trump's classroom, then this act is a means of exploring territory that other politicians fear to tread, and a means of altering the consciousness of the whole nation – a nation which, crucially, may not want to go back to class. It may well be that, as with advertising, a fantasy about politicians is preferable to the real thing.

TRUMP THE CHEERLEADER

> TRUMP: We need a leader that can
> bring back our jobs, can bring back our
> manufacturing, can bring back our military,
> can take care of our vets. Our vets have
> been abandoned.

> (APPLAUSE)

> TRUMP: And we also need a cheerleader.

A culture of success and individualism is also an
ideology. Mainstream politics has fallen into the
trap of seeing itself as a neutral arbitrating system
(or if it did not fall into a trap, it is because this
was its ideal from the start[16]). This is part of the
reason politicians must not offend or denigrate –
they are supposed to respect the moral autonomy
of their country's citizens. Trump breaks with all
this. He is not a politician, in fact or spirit – or even
ambition – and he makes no pretence otherwise.
Obama embodies the politician as a man burdened
with hard choices, trying to make sense of the
world and balance competing interests as best he
can. It is chillingly appropriate that the answer to
a near perfect politician, such as Obama, should

be someone so completely alien to politics. Trump does not attempt to make sense of the world. He does not work for the best outcome for all or fight for an ideal. Instead he ignores, discounts and abuses what it is in his interest to ignore and abuse, and his only explicit agenda is winning the election. Gone with Trump is the idea that one must not be partisan, or prejudiced.

This was a long time coming. The myth of neutrality, of a neutral government which allows citizens to make their own way, is easily hijacked by anyone who wants to limit government checks on their own power. Liberal neutrality, via Nozick[17], is a source for neoconservative pro-business ideology, whose voter base Trump is in the process of appropriating. The irony here is that it is support for that ideology Trump is undermining even as he reaps the rewards in his business ventures.

The condemnation of government tax has benefitted Trump twice: once by making him wealthier, once by letting him use that wealth to be the candidate that 'doesn't dig into people's pockets'. The democratic ideal and the ideal of the American politician was that of a timeless steward, safeguarder of freedom and non-judgemental of its citizens. Trump, by contrast, is utterly contemporary, proudly prejudiced, opinionated on everyone (they are either 'wonderful' or 'not good people'). The only thing he has in common with the archetypal politician is that he strives to be totally one-dimensional.

It is reason's greatest weakness to simplify in order to understand. Trump has operated the greatest reduction to date, simplifying the world into a binary of good and evil, perfectly mapped to the self and the other. Politics created a role which required an impossible psychology. Trump, with his apparent narcissism and fantasy, is uniquely able to fill that role.

TRUMP AS AMERICA

> TRUMP: When do we beat Mexico at
> the border? They're laughing at us, at
> our stupidity. And now they are beating
> us economically. They are not our
> friend, believe me. But they're killing us
> economically.
>
> The US has become a dumping ground for
> everybody else's problems.
>
> (APPLAUSE)

Trump refers to nations as if they were individuals:
nations 'beating' and 'killing' each other. This has
the benefit of redefining other nations as enemies
and refashioning the collective identity of the
United States. It also allows Trump to parallel
his business success as an individual with his
projected future success as President of the United
States.

He promises to look after American
interests in the way he looks after his own
interests. Correspondingly, Trump is unashamed of
being completely individualistic – looking out for
himself, destroying the competition and making

ever larger personal gains are the essence of his alleged greatness. This means that, in effect, Trump is asking the electorate to substitute America's interests for his own. He is asking us to believe that Trump is America. Trump, a success story of the American dream, is able to embody and replace that dream for those it has left behind.

It may be that Trump's chief talent is extending his inflated self-esteem onto the project he is working on. Whomever he happens to be working with, wherever his project happens to take place, and whatever the project is, is always 'wonderful', 'the best', 'talked about', 'important'. That importance is calculated by proximity to Trump. Trump's victories are proof that America is so starved for affection and adulation that it is willing to hand over money and executive power in return for them. Trump's offer is to do to the United States what he does to derelict properties – refashion them in his own image.

If money decides elections, then America is in the process of hiring a man to comfort it during its mid-life crisis. And the man most willing to take what's on offer is Donald Trump, a peroxide blonde who will act out every fantasy his client desires. America wants someone to tell it jokes and reassure it of its potency. America is tired of thinking.

TRUMP, VOICE OF THE PEOPLE

> TRUMP: So I've watched the politicians. I've dealt with them all my life. If you can't make a good deal with a politician, then there's something wrong with you. You're certainly not very good. And that's what we have representing us. They will never make America great again. They don't even have a chance. They're controlled fully – they're controlled fully by the lobbyists, by the donors, and by the special interests, fully.

Consider the dismissal by GOP strategist Rick Wilson of Trump supporters as "childless single men who masturbate to anime... these are not people who matter in the overall course of humanity."[18]

This elitist comment is a rebuttal to an article[19] comparing Samuel Francis' 1996 essay[20] 'From Household to Nation' to Trump's campaign. In that essay, Samuel Francis, an advisor to Pat Buchanan[21], recommends ditching 'conservative values' – free market, limited government and economic libertarianism – in favour of populist ethno-nationalism. It is a fundamental irony of Trump that in spite of being exactly the kind of businessman who benefits most from free markets and limited government, he is still being allowed to take the role of nationalist crusader against the global business elite.

From Rick Wilson's clear contempt for middle America, it is all too easy to see how at least one half of the American right is out of touch with the election-critical zeal that drives these 'childless single men' to support Trump so fervently. The conceptually uneasy alliance between economic and social conservatism (between the internationalist, pro-business neocons and the nationalist, Christian fundamentalists) is crumbling, with power shifting towards the nationalists. Amanda Taub goes so far as to suggest that 'we may now have a de facto three-party system: the Democrats, the GOP establishment, and the GOP nationalists'[22].

Samuel Francis in 1996 argued that huge swathes of the American population was being antagonised by both the left and the right. The left, spiritually, see Middle Americans as ignorant, savage bigots, and protect the interests of migrant communities. The right, economically, favour an increasingly unequal society and the cutting of Medicare and social security. Trump is mining an unlikely centre ground between these opposites.

Trump is the improbable spokesperson for an oppressed class – the white working class, which is the only class of people that can be demonised, ridiculed and discriminated against with near total impunity.

Their rates of drug abuse, alcoholism, obesity and suicide are rising, but the political voices that stand for their interests are heard through the distortion of race, religion and Nazi iconography. Trump, for all his vulgarity, is the politically moderate champion for an oppressed class, their Martin Luther King.

It is an unintended consequence of mass communication that a people's champion can be elected without their interests at heart, without a common background, and without any helpful policies. The spokesperson needs only to seem to oppose the oppressor class and promise to restore the dignity of the oppressed. From the view of the white proletariat, power shifts from Democrat to Republican and back without ever questioning the basic structures that sees it disempowered.

A tangential farce has taken place with Trump, who has become the representative of a disenfranchised group without actually communicating with them, except through certain rhetorical accidents. Language is the only thing that connects Trump with this untapped electorate and hence the Trump phenomenon really is a creation of language.

How did Trump end up as a snake in the nest of the Republican party? Perhaps because the views he held prior to the campaign fitted him better to the Democrats than to the Republicans. Trump's surprising history of liberalism – something seized upon by Ted Cruz's #NY Values campaign – includes being pro-abortion, being anti-guns and supporting the legalisation of drugs.

By catering to businessmen, the Republican party unwittingly allowed a non-conservative to seize the limelight and split the party. It would be a truly poetic inversion if Trump had indeed come to the aid of those marginalised by the Republican party – and terribly sad that he ditched all his inclusive values the moment they became inconvenient.

Trump has become the Frankenstein's monster of the Republican Party, their greatest triumph and their ultimate downfall. Not only is Trump taking support from other candidates and splitting his party, his increasingly reckless attacks on fellow Republican candidates from the February 13th GOP debate onwards, have come to dominate the whole Republican race.

His nicknames 'Lying Ted' and 'Little Marco' produced an equal and opposite reaction, with Rubio retorting 'you know what they say about men with small hands'. Even more controversially, Trump lays the Iraq War and 9/11 at the feet of the previous Republican President, George Bush. Trump dares to trumpet the view that the Iraq war was undertaken on false premises and that the American people were lied to – a view not uncommon outside of Washington but completely taboo within the Republican party.

Trump shows willingness to jeopardise the whole Republican enterprise in order to eviscerate his opposition and that willingness is a conduit for every popular opinion hitherto barred from mainstream politics.

Trump is a voice of the people, not in the spirit of social conscience, but in the spirit of competition – in that sense he is capitalism's answer to the socialist rally-leader: the free market's very own Che Guevara.

TRUMP AS GOD AND PALIN HIS DIVINE MESSENGER

Palin and Trump, surrogate parents for an orphaned generation. Palin bursts with passion at the podium in a nasal ecstasy while Trump looks on, a hulking colossus in a dark overcoat. He grimaces and nods, giving big dumb smiles and thumbs up.[23] Palin paints him as a giant, storybook figure. Palin is the heart and Trump the mind of this duumvirate, which came into existence on the 20th of January 2016 in the form of Palin's surreal, stream-of-consciousness endorsement of Trump, an almost dadaist mish-mash of nationalist and aspirational soundbites[24].

Travelling in a single rhetorical flourish from Whitmanesque inclusivity 'You farm families, and teachers, and teamsters, and cops, and cooks...' to the very beat 'You rock 'n' rollers. And holy rollers!' and then onwards into 80's romanticism with the Morrissean 'You with the hands that rock the cradle'. Palin, too, would have been a great subject for this book.

Palin is a kind of forerunner to Trump, a pioneer in the modern age of using rhetoric and nationalism to stir up the electorate. Correspondingly, she is relatively avant-garde in her language, which is ripe with metaphor and throws in bizarre catchphrases at odd moments. Her words are full of passion and, at times, poetry.

It is telling that Palin's relative passion and sincerity may well be what disqualifies her from reaching the heights that Trump scales. Next to her twisted eloquence and bursts of frantic, xenophobic humour, Trump appears astonishingly moderate and business-like. His rabble-rousing is that of the honest Joe stating his piece in court. His tone, when he fires off a ludicrously inflated statistic or pronouncement, is always sincere and matter-of-fact. Palin is the opposite, using deliberately overblown rhetoric. Where Trump might insert a well-placed controversy, Palin inserts a slogan or metaphor.

Palin bestows on Trump a dignity and authority – Trump is not 'of the people' as Palin is. Instead he appears in her speech as a kind of benevolent alien or semidivine messenger, fallen to earth from the planet of money. An Other who understands, and with his overblown success chutzpah, a kind of superman. Palin verges on biblical in her description: 'He says, 'I want you to succeed too.' And that is refreshing, because he, as he builds things, he builds big things, things that touch the sky, big infrastructure that puts other people to work'. Palin presents Trump as God. Intentional or not, in a race where the bible is the common text of the electorate, this kind of rhetoric is extremely apt.

Palin possesses an intuitive feel for explosive juxtaposition: 'In fact, they've been wearing a, this, political correctness kind of like a suicide vest.' This metaphorically links the political 'establishment' (or the left, or whoever her target is) with the great political bogeyman of terrorism. It's key to politicians like Trump and Palin that all their opponents form an amorphous mass. The same technique is employed to link the left with drug addicts: 'they take other people's money, and then their high is getting to redistribute it, right?'

Because Palin is more linguistically gifted (if that's the right word) than Trump, she is able to articulate more succinctly the implicit premise in a lot of Trump's positions and attitudes. First, that politics is run by a sinister and elitist cabal, which Trump is taking on: '*He's been able to tear the veil of this idea of the system*' – a phrase almost ambiguous enough to be true.

Consider this key passage, which reads like an illiterate manifesto:

PALIN: Trump's candidacy, it has exposed not just that tragic ramifications of that betrayal of the transformation of our country, but too, he has exposed the complicity on both sides of the aisle that has enabled it, okay? Well, Trump, what he's been able to do, which is really ticking people off, which I'm glad about, he's going rogue left and right, man, that's why he's doing so well. He's been able to tear the veil off this idea of the system. The way that the system really works, and please hear me on this, I want you guys to understand more and more how the system, the establishment, works, and has gotten us into the troubles that we are in America.

The permanent political class has been doing the bidding of their campaign donor class, and that's why you see that the borders are kept open. For them, for their cheap labour that they want to come in. That's why they've been bloating budgets. It's for crony capitalists to be able suck off of them. It's why we see these lousy trade deals that gut our industry for special interests elsewhere. We need someone new, who has the power, and is in the position to bust up that establishment to make things great again. It's part of the problem.

Immigration, the redistribution of wealth, elitism, the trade deficit and the collapse of American industry – these separable issues are crammed together so forcefully that the grammar of the sentences used to express them is shattered. Palin's cracked logic squeezes the nation's every problem into just over two hundred words. 'They are so busted, the way that this thing works.' Palin has freed herself from the constraints of grammar and is channelling pure reactionary – should I say revolutionary? – emotion.

And this is poetry: 'Right wingin', bitter clingin', proud clingers of our guns, our God, and our religions, and our Constitution.' Compared to this, middle class sensibilities really are sterile and bloodless. Compared to this, moderate language really is officious and dull. 'He's got the guts to wear the issues that need to be spoken about and debate on his sleeve' – is an almost Dylanesque subversion of idiom. 'The status quo has got to go' may be the pithiest couplet in revolutionary poetry.

It is in criticising the political elite for riding the 'gravy train' that Palin and Trump are most powerfully in sync. America's problems are blamed on the establishment in both parties, who prioritise campaign donations over ideas. Criticising Obama, Palin also demonstrates impressive grasp of the zeitgeist. 'He packs up the teleprompters and the selfie-sticks, and the Greek columns, and all that hopey, changey stuff and he heads on back to Chicago'.

She appeals to a reactionary part of all of us that denies modern culture. To Palin, the right wing is a beautiful thing, like a bird's wing. Further digging into Obama, she adds: 'a weak-kneed, capitulator-in-chief has decided America will lead from behind... kind of with the skills of a community organizer maybe organizing a neighbourhood tea'. By contrast, Palin and Trump appear warrior-like and strong. 'Like you all, I'm still standing', says Palin. In her audience's eyes she is a champion who has triumphed over politically correct society and the liberal media.

I'm as shocked and upset as anyone else to find myself part of a politically homogenous majority that despises and ridicules the fiery, radical, poetic hockey mom: an American Queen Boudica.

TRUMP THE CELEBRITY

> TRUMP: Wow. Whoa. That is some
> group of people. Thousands.

A sequence of non-sequiturs spills from the
colourless lips of the republican candidate,
the most abstract and grandiose of which are
transmuted by the magic of CNN into bold
headlines at the bottom of the screen: 'TRUMP:
I HAVE TO DO WHAT'S RIGHT'. A comment on
the GOP's reluctance to endorse him turns into
the assertion 'I AM A WINNER. I'M NOT LIKE
SO MANY OF THE OTHER PEOPLE YOU TALK
TO THAT ARE ESSENTIALLY LOSERS,' then
morphs without explanation into a passionate
condemnation of killers and extremists. It's
beautiful.

A public figure is an image on a television
screen, a voice on radio, a printed name, a meme
– but one you see more often than the name of
your mother or your closest friend. This is the
mechanism by which a leader in a mass society
can be said to have a connection with his or her
people. This is what lets him or her be known and
accountable – and electable – to all. Washington,
Westminster and Kremlin politics are rooted in

an age before the computer screen, or even the television screen. But modern politics has become a mass address, an infinite Gettysburg where an orator's technique converts every adversity into an incitement to patriotic violence. What does an oration look like, distended into a collection of sound-bites, repeating GIFs and bold-print headlines? It looks like a newsfeed, a sidebar of related articles or, in a person, Donald Trump.

But none of this is to say Trump is some kind of visionary or prophet, capable of reading his times. Trump is a product of his age not by nurture or intuition, but by natural selection. The Republican presidential hopeful of 2016 was always going to benefit from a Trumpian recipe, and Trump may only be the first symptom of a new politics.

Trump is living proof that in the age of mass media, nothing is of higher value than celebrity. Trump is the celebrity-king that our cult of adulation always hinted at but never quite dared to posit. Combined with the fact of reality television – the fact that stars can be 'famous for being famous' – you have the recipe for an unbounded, total personality, both at the top of our society and unaccountable to any of its definitions. In an ugly suit, with straw-like hair, Donald Trump has shuffled his shadowy bulk into the negative space of our new idolatry.

The 1990-2000 period of campaign management has been called the 'celebrity manager era'[25], when political advisors became more publically visible. The post-2010 period might be called the 'celebrity management era'. Trump was best known for playing the uncompromisingly hardnosed businessman in reality show The Apprentice. Looking at him now, it is not clear he ever stopped playing that role. Very possibly, Trump lives in the reality that reality TV pretends to capture.

We don't seem to have collectively realised how susceptible we are to images. Not only can Donald Trump use an image of confidence and certainty to completely nullify accusations of incompetence but, more severely, negative images can lead to irrational fear and bad decisions[26]. Why is terrorism so much more alarming to us than smoking, car accidents, drug abuse, tsunamis, global warming – than almost anything? Because its murders are compressed in time, and therefore capturable by the photographic lens.

Part of Trump's celebrity appeal, paradoxically, is that he is unattractive (in my opinion). Celebrity presidents have generally had some charm. You could easily imagine them starring as themselves in a political drama. But

Trump, with his eccentric looks, belongs where his celebrity started, in reality television.

This must be a part if what makes Trump appear 'down to earth' or 'one of us' in spite of his billionaire status and bizarre appearance.

Perhaps because his attempted simulation of attractiveness has so clearly failed – with his double combover, hair extensions and deep tan – we may assume that any other artifice he creates must also fail. We are tempted to think he may be speaking from the heart. In a way, this is correct. Trump is speaking from deep psychological urges in himself: his deep-rooted desire to provoke and impress is utterly genuine.

When Trump makes a claim, it is customary of him to use a precise type of claim: an exaggeration or anecdotal comment. His fame and fortune is built on making those kind of claims, whether they turn out to be true or false. The overblown statement is Trump's form of sincerity.

It is only when he attempts to be balanced, or clever, or complex, that we see artifice, because these are qualities he lacks and must therefore simulate. Trump has difficulty articulating the word 'but' – his pitch rises and his throat constricts around it and other qualifying words like 'probably'. In dialogue, Trump will repeat a phrase to himself again and again, as if trying to spark the chemical reaction that will produce his next explosive comment.

When Trump was a mere celebrity he probably wanted to appear urbane, sexy, powerful, unique. Instead he came across as buffoonish, ridiculous, idiotic – but yes, unique. Now he is a politician he attempts to appear decisive, competent, honest and powerful. Instead he appears impulsive, irresponsible, manipulative – but yes, powerful. And because the institution of democracy, which aims to translate public support into power instead translates perceived power into real power, the Trump phenomenon becomes possible.

The perceived dishonesty that the media both foists on and punishes politicians for has made political campaigning a kind of prolonged theatre performed for a massive, distracted audience. Public figures face the impossible task of being both totally transparent and totally inoffensive. Trump's celebrity means a way to break out of this paradigm by ignoring it. By staking out a position that was deliberately controversial and offensive from the beginning, Trump has given himself a mandate to speak for all the parts in the American subconscious that have been denied air time.

No longer bound by the moral preoccupations of his audience, Trump is allowed to pick whatever words occur to him. To continue a theatrical analogy, he is the equivalent of an untrained actor stunning audiences with artless sincerity. He speaks to a theoretical section of the electorate that is not politically aware, does not care too much about policy, has a simplistic view of politics and is unsympathetic towards political process and towards compromise.

He may be as contemptuous of the electorate as the educated middle classes are of him. By being totally cynical, Trump allows himself to be a kind of American idealist; a message of down-to-earth, working class vulgarity at last taking its rightful place as the heart of America, pumping its doctrine into the White House as an antivenom for white guilt.

Antecedent American demagogues include Rev. Charles Coughlin, Joseph McCarthy, George Wallace and Huey Long. None was ever as potent as Trump is now, arguably.

TRUMP, VOICE OF THE PEOPLE, PART II 'THE DEATH OF THE POLITICIAN'

> TRUMP: And, I can tell, some of the candidates, they went in. They didn't know the air-conditioner didn't work. They sweated like dogs.

> (LAUGHTER)

Trump does not speak in the same voice as your average political candidate – if it is unclear whether he believes the opinions he is expressing, it is because he is expressing soundbites, not opinions. This has been a long time coming. Barthes pointed out that when an author writes a simple statement in prose, it is unclear where that statement is supposed to be coming from[27] – is it folk psychology? Is it the view of a character? Of God? Of the author? Trump presents the same ambiguity. Is he a conduit for seething white rage? A casual and ignorant bigot? A delegate for big business, with its brand-speak and deliberate authority? A sleep talker dreaming the American Dream?

To borrow a Barthesian idea, language becomes substitute for a man[28]. By token of his unapologetic insincerity, Trump becomes free to channel every vernacular that serves his purpose – and each vernacular wins him a new set of supporters who may have nothing in common with each other. This gives him the cross-sectional appeal a presidential candidate needs, while also allowing him to reach out to hitherto unreachable communities. Not by understanding those communities, or translating their concerns into political language, but by the total opposite: completely forsaking political language and speaking in his own self-interest because self interest is the language of America. Self interest is the language of America and Trump is very interested in himself.

This is why the rise of Trump remains inexplicable to many. They look to the man for qualities which explain his success, but those qualities do not lie in him – they lie in what he has been allowed to represent, simply by being uniquely flexible as a mouthpiece. Trump does have personal qualities: he is rude, he is brash, he is callous. But more importantly, he is chosen.

It is not, as is often reported, that the public are somehow falling for his personal charm or charisma, or that they are suckers for a rash gesture. It is that Trump is being allowed to express the forbidden truths. Much as a prophet is said to access divine truth, Trump has accessed a commercial and political truth. By doing so he has struck a killing blow against all moral and factual truth.

So we can draw an analogy between Barthes' 'Death of the Author' and what we might call the 'Death of the Politician'. It is not Trump's history as businessman that qualifies him to the American people. It is not his gung-ho personality, his weathered face or his dreadful ambition. It is his role as adversarial candidate. Trump the politician is born simultaneously with Trump the candidate for the Republican nomination, appearing, as the papers like to say, 'out of nowhere' – he is a creature created by a political context. His origins outside that context are important only insofar as they allowed him step into the role that has defined him.

A sinister point of dis-analogy between the 'Death of the Author' and the 'Death of the Politician' is that an author's perceived lack of agency is theorised to empower readers, by restoring to them interpretive powers that a cult of authorship denies them. Not so with Donald Trump and his voters, engaging through an occult, one-way system that gives Trump access to support but gives supporters no access to or influence on his policies. Because Trump's language is free from the constraints policy and ideology would place on it, he is not bound by an electoral mandate.

TRUMP, VOICE OF THE PEOPLE, PT III 'TRUMPIAN ARGUMENT'

> TRUMP: So, just to sum up, I would do various things very quickly.

Trump does not speak in facts, figures or argument. He speaks in generalisation and anecdote, but in a way that is true to the way people think. The whole notion of politics as rational debate depends on a fair arena in which all participants, including the audience, attempt to follow the thread of the argument and where political actors who offend against reason are punished.

Trump has snipped away the idea that there is a thread of conversation, argument or debate upon which the rails of political discourse run. The fact that a sensible vote has not consolidated in opposition to Trump suggests an ugly truth: that the American people, and perhaps all people, are not sensible or reasonable. We are partisan, completely partisan, and more concerned with our man or woman winning the election than what happens when he or she does. In this, we are just like Trump.

There is a tendency to divide the rabid, irrational Trump supporter from the cynic who is choosing him as the beat-Hillary or beat-Bernie candidate. I think we are wrong to assume a sharp dividing line separating Trump and his fanatics from the rest of us. We act as if Trump's immorality and vulgarity somehow did not touch us, as if it were wholly separate from us.

But if Trump is elected, we are all to blame and we must look at ourselves, not pass the culpability on to some demonic mass whose opinion is intellectually and morally invalid. I do not intend this as a misanthropic or cynical dismissal, but it is not controversial to say that we collectively rely on general categories and make mistakes[29].

The secret to Trump's 'down-to-earth' reputation is simply that he approaches questions from the standpoint of generalisations like 'people are saying' or what is 'happening on the streets' or 'now what we're seeing with the Muslims'.

Statements like 'you have people who are mentally ill and no matter what you do they are going to come through the cracks' and 'we have people that are very sick walking the streets all over the place'[30]. These statements have a vagueness which is hard to directly contradict without recourse to a similarly vague counter-proposition, which is what makes Trump's vocal style so effective at drowning out reality.

Trump has repurposed his exaggerated business talk, with little modification, for politics. 'This will be the best golf course in the world' and 'the most talked about event of the week'. How can he know? It's not like they have contests. 'I would build a great wall and nobody builds better walls than me'[31]. This is an explicit Trumpian technique, as he outlines in *The Art of the Deal*: 'People may not always think big themselves, but they can still get very excited by those who do. That's why a little hyperbole never hurts... People want to believe that something is the biggest and the greatest and the most spectacular. I call it truthful hyperbole. It's an innocent form of exaggeration – and a very effective form of promotion.'

David Brooks argues that Trump takes his language from professional wrestling:

> From the moment he entered this presidential race, his campaign has been one long exercise in taking the 'low' manners of professional wrestling and interjecting them into the 'respectable' arena of presidential politics.[32]

When he brings his disregard for measurement to bear on things which do need to be measured (such as the economy), Trump gives birth to a new and powerful monster. His inexhaustible promises of the 'best' in everything are a fitting antidote to a culture increasingly dominated by technocrats and wielders of big data. To those left behind by the tech surge, to those who have not accepted Bill Gates as their king and Steve Jobs as their prophet, Trump may have a kind of barbaric, simple heroism.

Trump, in his subjective ignorance, is able to value the individual (namely, himself) above all systems and all processes. Not for him the age of increasing connectivity and awareness – Trump is a rich and powerful man who is not made anonymus by the flow of information. This allows him to be a kind of bastion, a rock in the ocean against progress. Fittingly, he is symbolised to the general public in the form of enormous skyscrapers: Trump Tower, Trump Plaza, Trump Parc, Trump Place – architecturally relics of a bygone, industrial America which was identified with its skylines.

This connection between Trump and America means that, in many ways, to dismantle the Trump formula you have to reject the American myth. You have to argue that salt-of-the-earth, hardworking, aspirational people are in no way better qualified for government than anyone else. You have to argue that the qualities of a ruler are not the qualities of a subject – and this is spiritually, if not logically, completely at odds with democracy.

Unsettlingly, many interviewers seem to give Trump an easy ride and seem happy to accept obviously fallacious arguments, anecdotal evidence and false generalisations, coming back to him with only the most half-hearted of objections which only give Trump an ever larger license to repeat and reemphasise his point, haloing himself in an ever-greater mushroom cloud of rhetorical fog. Without embarrassment he offers 'the most stringent laws are, in almost every case, [in] the worst places – it doesn't seem to work.'[33] *This is a bad argument.* He offers 'I would work very hard on mental health...' which doesn't mean anything, and its follow-up '... but I have to say, no matter what you do, you're gonna have problems' is an empty truism.

Trump consistently shies away on ever offering a theory. If faced with a difficult question, he invariably passes the intellectual burden: 'the theory is, they say this, if you have more guns, you have more protection'. He reserves his opinions for uncontroversial issues, such as his desire to win.

Consider this exchange:

> Statement: We have to a better job with mental health

Objection: What does that mean?
Reply: It means better services, better doctors, better reporting – there have been a couple of cases where the community have said 'we knew this guy for years.

Trump's response gently breaks a vague proposition into three equally vague propositions and one meaningless anecdote which rhetorically supports his anterior speech act but gives the conversational impression of having answered the objection. It may be an unworthy exercise, but Trump is good at it. You might object at this point that this could be applied to many politicians, which is absolutely true – but Trump serves well as the logical limit of this mode of engagement.

Another example: Trump in conversation with an NBC reporter. When she objects that research contradicts a statement he has made he simply replies 'Don't be naive. You're a very naive person ... you don't even know what you are talking about'[34].

During the same interview Trump ripostes, to a separate objection: 'number one I disagree with it, number two, whether it's true or not, illegal immigrants ... are causing tremendous crime'. This is of the form 'Whether P is true or false, P is true'.

This is a contradiction, but apparently it doesn't matter. The truth is irrelevant, the conversation goes on and Trump looks as strong as ever. Here's some anecdotal evidence of our own: an exchange between youtube user johnlocke445, presumably named after philosopher John Locke, and another user using the handle 'Nihilist'. If this doesn't demonstrate an uncanny cross-sectional appeal I don't know what does.

johnlocke445 5 months ago

I like this guy for one reason. He doesn't talk like a politician. He talks like my next door neighbor. What we don't need in Washington is another politician.

Reply · 680

Nihilist 6 hours ago

+johnlocke445 I'm a leftist and I like him because he's politically incorrect. I absolutely hate political correctness.

Case Study: Trump vs Cruz at the Fox Business GOP debate.

An incredible Trump-Cruz debate. To groans and laughter from the audience, Neil Cavuto fields Trump's spurious claim that Cruz might face a Democrat attack on his 'natural born' citizenship and hence his eligibility for the presidency. Cruz,

with jutting jaw and impeccable irony, observes
that John McCain and Mitt Romney, like him,
were perfectly eligible for president in spite of
not being born on US soil. He rebuffs Trump's
incoherent monologue to the contrary with airy and
contemptuous grace. As Trump speaks, inventing
poll numbers and insisting there is a question mark
where clearly there is none, you almost wish the
butchery of truth and reason could somehow put
a crack in his performance, but it is seamless. In
spite of the general conclusion by commentators
that Cruz seemed to have the upper hand in the
debate, Trump gets more applause and laughter
than anyone else in the room. Trump's loss to Cruz
at the Iowa primary was a brief olive branch in the
midst of despair.

TRUMP THE HATE PREACHER

> AUDIENCE MEMBER: We want Trump now.
>
> TRUMP: Our enemies are getting stronger and stronger by the way, and we as a country are getting weaker. Even our nuclear arsenal doesn't work.

Daniel Patrick Moynihan is often (falsely) credited with the saying 'everyone is entitled to his own opinions but not his own facts'. Not so in the case of Trump. He reveals that the veneer of rational debate and interests-of-all which Washington politics purported to work under was an illusion; a linguistic trademark for a ruling language which did its best to disguise its basis in power and populism. He reveals that with his highly effective use of dramatic claims to boost his popularity. The following is a list of Trump claims that turned out to be false.

Trump Claims (best of)[35]

1 *Thousands of Muslims in Jersey city celebrated the fall of the twin towers.*
2 *The Mexican government sends criminals across the borders.*

3 Most whites are killed by blacks.

4 Obama spent $25 million on a trip to New York.

5 American nuclear weapons don't work.

6 The White House is accepting 250,000 Syrian refugees.

7 The federal government sends refugees to Republican, not Democratic states.

8 'Real' unemployment is at 30%.

9 93 million people are out of work in the US.

10 The US is the most highly taxed nation in the world.

11 Syria's Christian refugees cannot enter the United States.

12 The Obamacare website cost $5 billion and doesn't work.

13 There are 30-34 million illegal immigrants in the United States.

14 ISIS built a hotel in Syria.

15 Ted Cruz has a double passport.

16 Most refugees are men, not women and children.

17 The families of the 9/11 hijackers were flown from the US to Saudi Arabia after the attacks.

18 Hillary Clinton started the Obama birth certificate controversy.

19 Only the US has birthright citizenship.

20 Public support for abortion is falling.

21 The US gets no oil from Libya.

22 *South Korea doesn't pay the United States for US troops.*

23 *The US is pledged to support Iran in an Iran-Israel conflict.*

On Politifact, the Pulitzer Prize-winning, fact-checking website, Trump has the worst rating of any politician[36].

Trump expresses incendiary opinions from a platform of authority in order to produce emotion and Clinton and others have followed suit, with Hillary making the unfounded claim that ISIS was using videos of Trump to gain followers – an untruth, but the right untruth and the one that opponents of Trump wanted to hear. This became a self-fulfilling prophecy, when a group (though not ISIS) did use Trump in a recruitment video[37]. Whether he wins or loses, Trump has already partially normalised his way of doing politics.

Nationalist demagogues are not a new thing, but they are a new thing in America, which for all its hawkishness is still politically built around the puritanical-come-spiritual rhetoric of the constitution, with its proud veneration of the founding fathers. The USA has given birth to not a screaming dictator but a guffawing one. One who plays not to the animalistic, Futurist fervour of a warlike race, but to a name-calling, jeering, cyberbullying instinct – the trolling instinct fostered in a mass society where the only way to be heard (your voice lost among the millions) is to be vulgar, to be shocking, to offend, to insult and to bait.

With the media forming the advance guard of this movement, pitting candidates against each other and reporting perceived slights of one celebrity to another, we have a modern form of communication between politician and electorate that only now is being exploited to the full.

Trump is the rarest of things, an agitator offering fundamental, one dimensional views who is also in all senses a pragmatist. Passionately offensive but not offensively passionate, he is like a soap opera character whose beliefs and attitudes inexplicably shift in the direction of maximum drama: Trump has cloaked himself in an atmosphere of constant rebellion, the constant adversary and rugged hero triumphing against limitless odds.

A choice quote: 'The other thing with the terrorists is that you have to take out their families, when you get these terrorists, you have to take out their families'[38]. This is often presented as a position Trump held and was later forced to backpedal on. But it is doubtful that Trump spent more time thinking over the issue than saying it.

Clearly, Trump knows his supporters are hungry for blood. Trump, most likely, is not far sighted enough to worry about who he alienates – he plays for local adulation, like a rock star, conquering one stage at a time and one of the biggest assets Trump has is an air of unstoppability. Indirectly this comes from loyal fans screaming his glory but primarily it comes in the person of Trump himself, scornful of anyone's opinion but his own.

When you have a person like Trump so close to government, things like the Geneva Convention or Hamdam vs Rumsfeld start to feel like pieces of paper or ancient history. I don't believe there's a benefit to picturing Trump as some kind of mad dictator, hypnotising the masses into destroying every institution that protects them – though by asking his supporters to swear fealty with a quasi-Nazi salute[3940], he invites the comparison. But the semi-serious response which is the due of every brutal, off-the-cuff Trump remark does suggest that he is warping, with his enormous mass (like a sun bending starlight) the political foundations of his country.

Trump candidacy speech revisited:
When Mexico sends its people, they aren't sending their best, they're not sending you, they're not

sending YOU. They're sending people who have lots of problems. And they're bringing their problems with us. They're bringing drugs, they're rapists, and some of them I assume are good people... I will build a great, great wall across our southern border and will make Mexico pay for that wall. Mark my words.[41]

Here Trump assigns villainous agency to Mexico but fails to ascribe a motive. He implies that there is a 'you' which Mexicans are not part of – even the good ones. There is an ironic grammatical error in 'they're bringing their problems with *us'*.

Uses 'and' instead' of 'but' in order to draw the venom out of the contradiction. Trump always uses 'and' instead of 'but'. Intentional or not, it serves to increase the illusion of simplicity. He acts as though he is the only man out there telling the simple truth as it is, but the truth is complicated, particularly on issues like immigration. Trump announces that Mexican immigrants are drug dealers and rapists, next to which the fact that 'some' of them aren't is easily brushed aside.

Trump rarely condescends to answer to facts that don't suit him. He simply gives them no emphasis and by the miracle of modern communications, these facts are drowned out by more radical statements. His final, astounding ambition to build a 'great, great wall' is biblical in proportion, ironic given his antipathy to China, and terribly cogent with his history of building garish, architectural monstrosities that bear his name.

Trump is playing both sides of the field, the inspirational 'anyone can be president' logic of hope and the paranoid 'our enemies are everywhere and a strong leader is needed' logic of fear, both as old as politics itself. They are especially effective in a mass democracy reliant on a limited number of media outlets[42]. Socrates was executed by means of the absurd, ambiguous and paranoiac claim that he was corrupting the youth. The father of all philosophy, mythically invincible in argumentation, was unable to persuade a jury of five hundred of his peers, convinced of his impiety by rumour and hearsay. This effect is amplified a millionfold in the case of Trump – he cannot be brought down by reason, and will remain as long as his image still has the power to drive his supporters to tears.

The US, too, uniquely combines hope and fear in its cultural offering. On the one hand, it is fiercely, constitutionally proud of its acceptance of all values. Yet there's a historical tendency towards exaggerated fear. A fear of a Catholic threat manifested out of alarmist reports of during the English Civil War in spite of a tiny Catholic population. There is a historic fear of secret societies – the Illuminati, the Masons, the spectral vanguards of a conspiratorial elite running the country. The fear of nuclear strikes during the Cold War is well within living memory. Trump stokes these religious, classist and international fears, often simultaneously. Trump's statements stand naked and alone, unsupported, unevidenced and extremely effective.

TRUMP THE MAN POSSESSED BY UNGOVERNABLE RAGE

'By trashing the United States and comparing his country unfavourably to himself, Trump tapped into something deep and powerful in the American psyche.'[43]

Gray and Montgomerie paint a demagogue Trump who reaches the disenfranchised electorate because his 'anger matches theirs'[44]. They are quite right to suggest that Trump is not a conventional politician and that he is riding a wave of post-crisis anger and revolt. But I don't think Trump is angry – does he seem angry? Trump is not able to tap into popular anger because he embodies it. What he taps into is every gripe and cliché he knows. Because he has been brought up on the same media as everyone else, what he knows is what the electorate knows. Truncate that sentence and we get: Trump knows the electorate.

This is no feat of visionary epistemology, it's simply that Trump is happy to ignore political commentators and does not imitate the views of politicians because he isn't one. One doubts he has ever really considered or understood the finer points made by his more sophisticated critics.

Ignoring political language, Trump defaults to common language, the language spoken by 'real' Americans. In that language, the most obvious provocations are the most resonant.

Trump's targets could not be more obvious – Mexicans (exploiting racial tensions), Muslims (exploiting religious tensions) and millionaires (exploiting class tensions). Virtually any sentence in his populist dialect passes as 'down-to-earth', compared to the diplomatic, theatrical language of mainstream political discourse. In this theatre, anger, legitimate or illegitimate, is redirected to fuel Trump. His skin is darkening to unfathomably deep shades of ochre as it is pumped with his audience's vicarious aggression, and Montgomerie sets aside some time to comment on 'his vanity, his face lifts, his fake hair'[45].

The anger Trump is channelling is a catch-all answer to globalisation, intellectual elites, financial crises and minority politics. It is not a sensible answer, or even a remotely convincing one. But it is an answer nevertheless. The loss of American prestige caused by its disgraced-yet-untoppled financial industry and it's failed-yet-continuous intervention abroad is transformed into anger then redirected at the people those crises harmed the most. Trump is a triumph of American self-denial, a seductive refusal of all agency in its own cultural downfall.

But those who criticise Trump fall into the same error, blaming his vulgarity and offensiveness on him personally. Trump would never have taken such extreme views if the moderate majority had not alienated and polarised huge segments of the population. The very fact that we are so terrified of a Trumpian president is a symptom of the revulsion and hate we quietly hold towards our own people. The Trump voters are right about one thing: the foreign and financial crises of recent years were not caused by grassroots radicalism in government. The fact that Trump offers no solution, or would do worse, does not undo this fact. Trump is riding the winds of change.

Still, it may be to Trump's credit that he is able to take adulation as strength, without being intimidated by opposition and ridicule. To focus on the positive and underplay the negative is what is taught by almost every self-help book and therapy course. Trump, by taking this to the extreme, becomes the logical limit of our well-intentioned effort to better ourselves. Trump shows that to be a independent, healthy, strong, motivated human being with a positive attitude is not necessarily an uncontroversial ideal.

Trump is able to be powerful because he is a rupture in a culture where individual autonomy can be safely maximised, because it is assumed that individuals making free choices will not destroy the system that guarantees their autonomy. This faces the well-known criticisms that free markets are unequal, that community is being destroyed by atomism, that the environment is being violated by unchecked consumption and so on. It faces a fresh criticism in the person of Donald Trump. If autonomy and morality do not coincide and if a politician's display of autonomy has political power in itself, then the whole political system risks being subject to a politician's individuality. In that case, the role of the politician is no longer to serve the community (or polis) – it is to express himself as an individual.

Trump does not make a distinction between acting in his private interest and acting for the good of the community. This proposition, filtered though untechnical and opinionated language, is his brand and he is loved for it. In other words, he directly benefits from not caring at all about his community, or the system he is engaged in. He is the answer to the apathetic citizen – an apathetic politician. And this really spells the end of politicians as we know them.

You could also argue that a dark element in American democracy has crept its way up into its elected officials, such that they cease to act as stewards and representatives for an electorate. Instead they continue to 'vote' – to choose in their own interests. Their relationship to their supporters becomes like that of mirror instead of that of a representative. A voter is supposed to vote according to his beliefs, or in his own interest – a free vote, not subject to any external notion of what is right and wrong. This is the essence of democracy. Trump, likewise, acts out his own preference – which is to get elected. Seeing her essence in him, democracy raised him as a champion. In return, Trump replaced democracy – with himself.

We can connect this excess of individualism with that rage Freddy Gray identifies in the American people – but I suggest this rage primarily fuels a narcissistic denial of criticism. Trump is able to transform criticism and insecurity into motivation and power through the medium of rage and vanity because he is motivated to preserve an ideal self-image. Trump effectively offers his own psychological strategies to the whole of America, with devastating results. This may be an inevitable symptom of a culture which permits and even promotes those tendencies.

With the advent of Trump, individualism can no longer be seen as neutral and with it, the language of professional America can also no longer appear neutral: it must carry the taint of an amoral egomania. Every inflated credit report, overly officious CV, fantastical business proposal, trite entrepreneurial slogan and inflated elevator pitch is to blame for the Trump phenomenon: these are the constituent elements in an enormous backdrop of insincerity and bravado that allows Trump to flourish, and for which he may be rewarded with the highest office in the land.

We see the same infirmity in *X-Factor* contestants quivering under the gargantuan Trump-ego of the celebrity judge, or first-time interviewees fumbling grandiose Trump-phrases, too huge and phallic for their innocent mouths. We see it in small business owners submitting some crackpot, Trump-ambitious investment proposal, conceived in panic at midnight – and worse, we see it when that proposal is granted.

We see it when bloggers and self-help gurus bullet-point the ladder to human perfection, offering as solutions to every emotional crisis the twin strategies of positive thinking and surrounding oneself with supportive 'positive people' (but never critical, 'negative' people). What kind of motivational speaker invites you to question whether your feelings of self-hate and anxiety may exist because you are a vain, stupid egotist that doesn't know what he's doing? That is a possibility we are invited to reject in every circumstance as unhelpful. Magnified on a societal scale, an American scale, a global scale, it is a source for the cultural blind spot which spawned Trump and those like him.

TRUMP THE BUSINESSMAN

> TRUMP: We have all the cards, but we don't know how to use them. We don't even know that we have the cards, because our leaders don't understand the game.

In startling contrast to Trump's cavalier, coarse style, emissions from his companies and spokespersons are always written in impeccable business language. Strangely enough, this language, common to all professional PR, follows the Trumpian formula. Slogans are wheeled out in accessible yet pompous language designed to engender trust and confidence.

Trump University has these pearls of advice: 'Our mission is to teach you success.' 'We've been here since 2005, and we're always looking ahead.' 'We believe people absorb more efficiently and faster when they learn by doing.' 'What we're proudest of: Giving people the knowledge they need to succeed.'. A language that veers so close to meaningless that it almost collapses in on itself, somehow held together by the smell of money – which is as good a definition of the Trumpian vocabulary as I am likely to invent. The trick of vacuous, aspirational mantra, slightly modified to serve the confrontational atmosphere of the election campaign, has served Trump well. Democracy and private business are not the same thing. They have been linked in our consciousness, particularly in the United States, but their origins and imperatives are wholly distinct. The 1930's association between emotion and private enterprise in America – the paternal figure of General Motors, the agony aunt cosmetics, the rebellious record labels – is parallel to the elevation of the head of state to patriarch in Stalinist Russia and Nazi Germany. It is private business, not government, that created modern America and the consumer lifestyle. It is a phenomenon that completes a symbolic full circle with Trump, a complete fusion of businessman and patriarch, who goes so far as to advertise Trump products during campaign rallies, as if Trump and his goods were one and the same[46, 47].

Behind the mantra of pro-business, limited government is the idea that business can satisfy desires and maximise utility in a way that politicians cannot. Trump, as a businessman and politician, is an answer to that, acting simultaneously as business advocate and champion of the people. The possibility that business and public may have different interests does not seem to occur to him.

American society has attempted to empower its citizens via their buying desires. This has disempowered the politician as focus-point and expression of those wishes. A politician is as beholden to the consumer as anyone else, since the consumer is also the voter. The domain of consumer desire left for the politician, once private businesses have feasted off sex, power and fashion through cigarettes, motorcars and high street retail, is the desire for nationalist identity, for an enemy and for justice.

Trump offers the electorate a chance to satisfy these desires, by advertising himself and offering himself as a consumable brand. The advert is his aspirational, rebellious, strongman rhetoric and florid promises. The purchase is the vote. Democracy created the election campaign and capitalism created the consumer fad and their combination created Trump.

America is the first country where a purchase became, rather than a way of getting what you need, or what you want, a way of expressing yourself. This is why purchases are manipulable by glamorous ads and celebrity endorsement. It may now also be the first country where the vote is closer to a fashion statement than a political act, because the primary role of a modern American is that of consumer, not citizen. Votes are a natural resource to be harvested by politicians like Trump. Trump is no more interested in making America great than he is in golf courses in Scotland or hotels in Vegas. Winning the election, for Trump, might even amount to no more than a four-year license to promote his business interests using the executive arm of government. If Trump wins the election and turns out to be a crook, then that really is the death of the American Dream because its ideal citizen turned out to be a con man. If he wins the election and abandons business to pursue the prophet-like character his followers have invented for him, the danger may be worse still.

Trump the businessman may well be a good blueprint for Trump the elected official. Consider the following story:

> In 1990, after an analyst at Janney Montgomery Scott said that Trump's Taj Mahal project would initially 'break records' but would fail before the end of that year, Trump threatened to sue the firm unless the analyst recanted or was fired. The analyst refused to retract the statements, and was fired by his firm. Taj Mahal declared bankruptcy for the first time in November 1990. A defamation lawsuit by the analyst

against Trump for $2 million was settled out of court. The analyst's statements regarding the Taj Mahal's prospects were later called 'stunningly accurate'. [48]

Ironically, however, Trump's success in the polls correlates negatively with the commercial value of his brand.[49]

TRUMP THE ADOLESCENT

From Mark Bowden's Vanity Fair article, December 10th of 2015:

> 'Trump struck me as adolescent, hilariously ostentatious, arbitrary, unkind, profane, dishonest, loudly opinionated, and consistently wrong. He remains the most vain man I have ever met. And he was trying to make a good impression. Who could have predicted that those very traits, now on prominent daily display, would turn him into the leading G.O.P. candidate for president of the United States?'

In retrospect, how did we not see it coming? Trump has done something no politician has ever dared do, which is be ostentatiously wrong. He has taken what was a drawback of political life – having your imperfections placed under a magnifying glass – and turned it into his greatest asset. Most politicians shy away from the camera or put on a front of impossible perfection that cannot possibly be sustained. Trump wears his ugliest features on his sleeve. He is proud to be arrogant, proud to be rich, proud to make unsupported claims, proud like America is proud, like her biggest industries and brands. In a year where you have the world's hottest male actors playing avaricious hedge fund managers as heroes[50] it seems the transformation of vice into virtue in American culture is finally complete.

Bowden continues:

'He has no coherent political philosophy, so comparisons with Fascist leaders miss the mark. He just reacts. Trump lives in a fantasy of perfection, with himself as its animating force.'

This is key to understanding Trump: his acting out of a fantasy. This is what Trump has in common with Lady Gaga, David Bowie, Snoop Dogg and Rimbaud – he lives in a fantasy of excess and success and invites ordinary Americans to live it with him. Instead of presenting the American Dream as an aspiration, he presents it as an established fact. His is an uncontaminated conservatism, the willing delusion that the system works and that our way of life is ethically sound. Hence his reflexive, confident dismissal of every fact that contradicts this fantasy. It is every bit as astonishing as the Bowie donning nail paint and lipstick, the Sex Pistols displaying the Nazi flag or Morrissey wrapping himself in the Union Jack. Trump is unabashedly offering a myth that does not have to be true, or right, or achievable, or real. It just has to be compelling.

Bowden's article reads worryingly like the tale of tyrannical excess you might expect in Hollywood renditions of a drug emperor or porcelain dictator. Trump's private life is rife with arbitrary exercises of power, gross displays of wealth and a pathological need to impress. Is this any surprise, given our tendency to mythologise and elevate personalities according to how demonstrably they live in their own reality and how far that reality departs from the norm?

This, at least, is not uniquely American. The 'visionary', the Raskolnikov-Napoleon who is able to transcend the ordinary on strength of a personal hallucination, has always been held as the tip of the spire in human possibility. Tales of a pop star or entrepreneur's diva behaviour, their obsession with control, is always assumed to be a part of their unique genius.

Bowden paints Trump as an adolescent. But for the most part Trump has merely acted out the self-help advice that is freely and injudiciously dispensed wherever you look. We are instructed in how to be yourself, how to believe in yourself, how to not care what others think, how to be motivated, how to succeed, how to make money. 'The Donald' does not simply benefit from integral human myths, he has the spiritual affirmation of every blog post, self-help book and advice column that offers simplistic and general advice. We exchange general statements in order to understand each other and therefore, to many, what Trump says seems to make sense. 'Without passion, you don't have energy. Without energy, you have nothing. Nothing great in the world has been accomplished without passion'[51].

You can accuse Donald Trump of many things, but you cannot accuse him of being without passion, without energy or without direction. The world is such that many of us feel we lack that superficial trinity. If our need is translated into a grossly uninformative language that promises all and says nothing, we have created a placeholder for someone, anyone, to gather power by exploiting our insecurities. Consider the cult leader, the guru, the industry seminar's keynote speaker. When such a language is communicated on a mass scale, such that it takes a life of its own, it can place even someone as unqualified as Donald Trump in the driving seat of anything, including American government.

TRUMP THE ARTIST

> TRUMP: Now, our country needs – our country needs a truly great leader, and we need a truly great leader now. We need a leader that wrote *The Art Of The Deal.*

> AUDIENCE MEMBER: Yes.

The Art Of The Deal, the book that Trump claims is the #1 best selling business book of all time, contains the germ of almost every personality trait and every technique that has characterised his candidacy.

The opening salvoes of Trump's magnum opus make the most of his unstructured, entrepeneur-adventurer lifestyle, which, crucially, involves no accountability or rules. The tragic thing about reading about Trump's day to day is that you get the impression that nobody is really on Trump's side, because his interlocutors are always business interests and potential targets.

Trump lives in a nightmare of the deal, where every interaction is a means to achieving the stalemate that benefits him most. He does not seem to know how to work *with*, but he well knows how to work *against*. His is a John Wayne, Lone

Ranger aesthetic (though ostentatious rather than stoic).

His business transactions appear based on hearsay 'word is out on the street that I've been a big buyer' – the same clichés that bolster his political opinions. The justificatory tools that let Trump take the risks that make him his big deals (and saw him file four bankruptcies between 1991 and 2009) are put to work in his political message, with barely any alteration. There is always a 'word out' and there is always the opinion of the 'best guy in the business'.

The book is relentlessly self-aggrandising. It would seem that Trump won every lawsuit and tennis match he ever engaged in. Everyone that ever agreed with him was 'nice' or even 'wonderful'. Everyone that ever disagreed with him (or sued him) was 'totally incompetent' or 'pompous'. The only time Trump is ever wrong is when he underestimates the media attention and good will his projects are due. You can't pin this totally on Trump: every self-help book benefits from self-assurance and the illusion of authority.

The Art Of The Deal is at least honest in that it does not hide its boastfulness behind a veneer of compassion or humility. *The Art Of The Deal* is a shameless advert and ego-shrine for Donald Trump

– but of course in Trump's world, adverts and ego are all good.

He regales the reader with tales designed to impress. We are lavished with free theatre tickets, private tennis courts, intimidations of the opposition by telephone, but the one thing he seems to consider most impressive is excess. *'Finally, I see a huge and magnificent gold wreath for the entrance to the building, and decide we should use just that. Sometimes – not often, but sometimes–less is more.'*

Trump takes the adage 'less is more' and shifts it in pitch such that 'huge and magnificent' corresponds to 'less'. Trump speaks in clichés – they constitute the spiritual part of his limited vocabulary – and applies them in his fantasy world, however absurd the distortion of meaning, in an attempt to seem both eccentric and wise. The fact that two qualities might be conceptual opposites is, for him, never a problem. He is, to his great credit, completely free from analytical and critical hang-ups.

Trump emerges in *The Art of The Deal*, written when he was nearing 40, as a kind of social Darwinist. He views the world as an irrational jungle where the most successful people are tough, masculine and neurotic . His (erotic?) aim is simply to beat those people *'I love to go up against those guys, and I love to beat them'*. Trump has not made the political promise to serve his constituents. He clearly and unapologetically intends to serve himself. Politics, too, is a game to win by beating competitors. Trump approaches politics with the aim of beating other politicians, and then beating other nations – he is not there to safeguard shareholders, investors or citizens.

Given Trump's record of failure to safeguard his shares and investments, this is somewhat alarming and it remains to be seen how far politics, like other disciplines, will fall prey to selfish competition among its practitioners. It is crucial that Trump's emphasis is on the DEAL, an aggressive, instant, penetrative act which decides success or failure. He has no time or interest – or, one suspects, understanding – of conservation, sustainability, let alone 'right'. If life for Trump is split into deals, then life for Trump is not a continuous narrative. Trump's world is not made of plural interests which must find compromise. The world is not nor should it be en route to greater stability. Instead life is a series of conflicts, each of which is measured as a defeat or victory.

Trump is free of the 'big picture' – all the epistemological, ethical and logistical problems that the human race laments having failed to solve, or denounces as insoluble. Trump wholeheartedly embraces the solution of ignoring them in order to keep his eye on the win. Under the subtitle *Maximise Your Options* he writes 'I never get too attached to one deal or approach', which explains Trump's inconsistent policies and viewpoints, and his otherwise unaccountable pride in that inconsistency.

Trump is also committed to the idea that his instincts are a better guide for what is right than facts, statistics or measurable trends. *'I don't hire a lot of number-crunchers, and I don't trust fancy marketing surveys. I do my own surveys and draw my own conclusions'*. This may not be a terrible choice to make as an individual – we do not all have to live according to the sterile and sexless mandates of economics. But a country is not a person, thought Trump treats it as one. A country must be interpreted through facts and statistics, the unfathomable diversity of its millions of people and the events that affect them.

Trump's claim to greatness is that he 'thinks big'. The reality is that he talks big and thinks simple. Building a golf course in Scotland he remarks 'I hope I'm given the chance to do something really terrific for Scotland'. This campaign-style sentence was already a staple of his business bravado. At this point, a superlative in the mouth of Trump has no meaning, it is pure ornamentation. I contend that Trump thinks small, very small. He never lets himself be distracted by concerns beyond his next foray – what the ramifications would be if he banned Muslims from entering the US, who he might offend by making a sexist remark. Much less does he appear to worry about whether he is doing right or wrong. Trump is focussed on impressing people, which is the smallest and pettiest aspiration we have – but it is one we all have. Freudian psychologist would be tempted by his size fixations. *'Before I get off, I also put in a plug for NBC's locating its offices in the world's tallest building. 'Think about it,' I say. 'It's the ultimate symbol.'*

Finally, *The Art Of The Deal* does contain one nugget of wisdom that Trump should probably pay more attention to: 'You can't con people, at least not for long. You can create excitement, you can do wonderful promotion and get all kinds of press, and you can throw in a little hyperbole. But if you don't deliver the goods, people will eventually catch on.'

TRUMP THE PHILOSOPHER

TRUMP: You know, all of my life, I've heard that a truly successful person, a really, really successful person and even modestly successful cannot run for public office. Just can't happen. And yet that's the kind of mindset that you need to make this country great again.

So ladies and gentlemen...

(APPLAUSE)

I am officially running...

(APPLAUSE)

... for President of the United States, and we are going to make our country great again.

(APPLAUSE)

From *The Art Of The Deal*: 'Money was never a big motivation for me, except as a way to keep score.' We may worry that Trump treats politics as a game, is indifferent to the needs of the electorate and cares only about winning. But we must concede that his is an approach true to the vogue for data and measurable success. In modern culture, all things unquantifiable face a double pronged attack, on one side from the big data analysis that increasingly governs business decisions, on the other from the goal-setting pulp wisdom in advice columns and self-help books. This doesn't have to be a bad thing: the best companies are often the ones that handle data best, and it is true that objectives can only be accomplished if they are first defined.

It becomes a bad thing in the hands of a figure like Trump who identifies completely with numbers like his worth in dollars and the height of his buildings. Trump has abandoned our reality and is interested only in how a certain set of statistics, be it net value in dollars, share price, or votes, relates to another set – the relative stats of his competitors, be they business tycoons, shareholders or politicians. Trump thrives in an environment of measurement – be it delegate count or hand size. For Trump, any natural notion of success has become subservient to the means used to measure it, which is a risk for all value systems.

With his mania for competition, Trump has inadvertently put his finger on relativistic attitudes towards reality which we confront in academic discourse. The incommensurable task of resolving conflicts between communities with different values and the impossibility of knowing the status of one's own values are conceptual sophistications totally lost on Trump. But whether he knows it or not, by choosing to measure himself only in relation to his nearest competition, he has come down heavily on the side of relativism and hence modernity. His moral attitude, however, is the complete opposite of relativism. In his judgements of others, Trump is a card-carrying absolutist.

From *The Art Of The Deal:*

> There are people – I categorize them as life's losers – who get their sense of accomplishment and achievement from trying to stop others. As far as I'm concerned, if they had any real ability they wouldn't be fighting me, they'd be doing something constructive themselves.

This argument suggest that Trump's opponents are losers, and has the added benefit of being applicable to any confrontation. The fact that Trump himself must inevitably be involved in confrontations where his opponents could say the same thing of him is not something he appears to consider.

This mantra of ferocious positivity should entail moral predicaments where proactive actions by different individuals do not coincide, leaving one at an impasse requiring political resolution. But it would be fatal to Trump's whole way of life to entertain this possibility. Trump's doctrine requires that his moral positivity be somehow exclusive to him – and if he is to navigate the world using that philosophy, then it must be immoral, or at least demoralising, to think from another person's perspective.

This result treats empathy as immoral and is another instance of Trump's inversion of reality – counterpart to his transubstantiating greed and ambition from cardinal sins into cardinal virtues. A world-view that only has room for one direction of success is also indicative of a vestigial childhood narcissism, incapable of separating world and self.

What is the content of the Trumpian category of winners and losers? I contend it can only be a moral category. It does not matter how rich his opponent, how great his accomplishments, his respect in the community – if he has the temerity and lack of vision to challenge Trump, he is a loser. This is a labelling of the opponent as an enemy of progress: a small-minded individual whose self-worth is parasitic on the self-worth of others.

The 'loser' is a kind of inverse human who thrives on the difference between how successful others could have been and how successful they are. Apart from the psychological implausibility of such a character, it is a startling feature of this view (which is by no means unique to Trump) that it posits an ethical being whose ethics are the complete inverse of Trump's. Losers thrive on Trump's lack of success, while he thrives on his plenty of success. Trump is therefore locked in a zero-sum game with all his opponents, the 'losers'; a zero-sum game with self-esteem as the prize.

Trump's moral system is completely based on Trump's interests and the category of evil, which we might want to fill with things like racism, hate and hypocrisy, is instead filled by the 'losers' who oppose Trump. This morality of success conveniently demonises the vast majority of the human population and removes all moral obligations on those better off. America is a community which relates to itself through idealisation, which is why it is vulnerable to a self-idealiser like Trump, whose ethical code unreservedly directs him in the direction of maximum triumph.

But Trump may be a victim as much as anyone else here. His pastor was Norman Vincent Peale, author of *The Power Of Positive Thinking.* This book (tagline 'You Can If You Think You Can') does its best to destroy the separation between fantasy and reality, insisting that a positive attitude can solve anything. It has been criticised for being full of hard-to-substantiate anecdotes and rejecting self-knowledge, for encouraging a black-and-white view of life that is characteristic of psychiatric disorder, for exaggerating the fears and negativity of the reader and for associating all negative feelings and conditions with guilt. Trump's morality is shaped by the crude and individualistic logic of aspiration from the start.

This mantra is more or less what the successive generations of the information age have been brought up to believe. We now see it reflected back to us in the image of one man, Trump. Excessive belief in 'the power of positive thinking' might be the psychological mechanism that enables Trump to propose ridiculous and ill-conceived policies, confident that if the attitude behind them is good, they will somehow work out. 'Make America Great Again' really is the worst kind of empty aspirational slogan – it fails to set the parameters of greatness, while the path to greatness becomes whatever the candidate with the slogan in his or her mouth says it is. It's a hollow slogan but one which politics is practically defenceless against.

An example of Trump's moral onanism: 'I think if I do something wrong, I think, I just try and make it right. I don't bring God into that picture.'[52] And in response to Pope Francis' non-specific comment 'A person who thinks only about building walls, wherever they may be, and not building bridges, is not Christian', Trump retorts 'For a religious leader to question a person's faith is disgraceful'[53]. This evinces a strong belief in his own moral authority, but what is more remarkable is how he goes on to invite his audience to share his ethical autonomy, proclaiming that 'no leader, especially a religious leader, has the right to question another man's religion or faith'.

Not content with mere theological showboating, he goes on to weave Pope Francis into a conspiracy on the part of the Mexican government with Trump as the target and warns that only Trump stands between the Vatican and ISIS. This is Trump's now-standard response to perceived slight; an instinctive coordination of the three arms of his provocative platform – immigration, the elites and terrorism – to mount an unnecessarily aggressive defence which garners massive media coverage. The case is also typical of the media's fanatical compulsion to pit political celebrities against each other, a compulsion Trump has exploited ruthlessly.

This is the defining syllogism of Trumpian philosophy:

Proposition: Success is determined by self-belief.

Proposition: Self-belief is morally right.

Conclusion: Success is moral. (Corollary, failure is sinful).

In the world of Peale/Trump, it is moral to believe in yourself. Hence, if you believe in yourself, you are 'right' – and from here it is a very short (and very irresponsible) step to: if you believe in yourself, then what you believe is true. This is how we reach Trump's fantasy world, from which we can extrapolate the whole fantasy of the American reification of the individual.

TRUMP THE FANTASIST

> TRUMP: We need somebody that can take the brand of the United States and make it great again. It's not great again. We need – we need somebody – we need somebody that literally will take this country and make it great again. We can do that.

Michael Kinsley very helpfully points out that the moment we started treated Trump's jibes as analysis-worthy positions and propositions, we were sucked into that fantasy world where Trump's rhetoric is the simple truth and you can solve any problem with the right attitude. This attitude-reifying attitude, I have suggested, is inestimably widespread in all industries and walks of life.

Kinsley reports: 'The press is so hostile to Trump that it has broken new ground in what reporters are allowed to say in ostensibly 'objective' news articles and broadcasts. Even Richard Nixon, the man who kept an 'enemies list' that included reporters he was going to get even with, was treated with more respect. But every insult from the hated media just makes Trump stronger.'[54]

This is Trump's greatest gift: a fantasy life and narcissism so strong that the whole political dialogue is drawn in its wake. Trump buried the gap separating clown, politician and demagogue with phrases so vulgar, offensive and damaging that he had to be taken seriously. Once he was taken seriously, we accepted a little bit of his fantasy into our political structure and collective consciousness, where it spread like a virus. It also directed focus away from Trump's absurdity and onto his 'policies'.

We spend our time attacking the ludicrous spectres of policy – time Trump did not spend – and they stand between Trump and genuine criticism. Each outrageous 'policy' takes the fire instead of Trump, wins him support, and is ultimately retractable. The political energy that should have gone into dismissing him has instead been used to set him up as a kind of antichrist. But the reality, as Kinsley puts it, is that:

> 'Trump has no 'plan' for anything. He just has a mouth ... Looking for some kind of ideological thread in Trump's various positions is a fool's errand (and another victory for Trump). The appeal of Trump's alleged views on every issue is their extremeness. That, and their seeming

simplicity. The fact that he hasn't thought them through and has more or less pulled them out of the air (or out of his ass, as Trump himself might put it) is a feature, not a bug, as they say in Silicon Valley. Trump stands for the proposition that you don't need to know much to run the government. You just need to use your common sense and to grow a pair, as Sarah Palin so memorably advised.'

Kinsley also observes that the populist appeal of Trump rises with his ability to ignore reality through the medium of lavish, empty promises.

Trump sets no limit on the achievable, something we are all advised to do by inspirational slogans and aspirational memes. He does not admit that there must be compromise and this is extremely seductive. Our media are limited in their ability to dissect issues and much better at simplifying them, so the image we get of Trump is not fractured as it should be. He is allowed to express an impossible policy in a merely false sentence, and thus expand the political language in the direction of the fantastical.

Kinsley observes that if we view America as an individual, it is an immature individual, unable '...to acknowledge as a nation what we accept and deal with in our personal lives, which is that *more of this means less of that*.' This America-individual sounds a lot like Donald Trump, or any other bombastically motivated entrepreneur. The fact that Trump resembles his country through psychological immaturity may go a long way in explaining why his crude fantasies are so able to sway the electorate. It is also suggests why Trump's success is so threatening to the whole idea of America and democracy.

TRUMPINARIUM

Trump, hands hanging limply off the arms of his chair. Behind him, a wall plastered in blue TRUMP signs. A nervous interviewer makes high pitched, perfunctory challenges, allowing Trump to sweep his points away with increasing fervour. The chin comes down, dividing the face like an enormous auburn sack and Trump peers from under ginger eyebrows as his interlocutor fields a nervous criticism.

Here follow a selection of 'Trumpinaria' – quotations from, comments on and descriptions of Donald Trump. I hope the reader will enjoy matching each comment to its corresponding 'Face of Trump'.

TRUMP: What's the difference between a wet raccoon and Donald Trump's hair? A wet raccoon doesn't have seven billion fucking dollars in the bank.

TRUMP: I am officially running (lower jaw comes forward to reveal small, sharp teeth) for President of the United States (lips purse coquettishly) and we are going to make our country great again (eyebrows rise, as if telling a joke).

TRUMP: The beauty of me is that I'm rich.

TRUMP: My Twitter has become so powerful that I can actually make my enemies tell the truth.

TRUMP: Donald J Trump is calling for a total and complete shutdown of Muslims entering the United States. Until our country's representatives can figure out what the hell is going on.

TRUMP: I will build a great, great wall across our southern border and I will make Mexico pay for that wall. Mark my words.

TRUMP PLACARD: 'The silent majority stands with TRUMP'

MICHAEL M. BLOW: He is odd and entertaining, vacuous and vain, disarming and terrifyingly dangerous.[55]

TRUMP (On John McCain): He's a war hero because he was captured. I like the war heroes who aren't captured.

TRUMP: You know it doesn't really matter what the media write as long as you've got a young, and beautiful, piece of ass.

TRUMP: My IQ is one of the highest – and you all know it! Please don't feel stupid or insecure, it's not your fault.

TRUMP: The concept of global warming was created by and for the Chinese to make US manufacturing non-competitive.

TRUMP (reading in response to the Syrian refugee crisis): 'Oh shut up, silly woman,' said the reptile with a grin. 'You knew damn well I was a snake before you took me in.'[56]

MEXICAN LABOURER: Donald Trump? That son-of-a-bitch who says we're all thieves? Look, son-of-a-bitch, how we rape these stakes (hammers stakes in a construction site). How we work ourselves to death just to eat. I make $1,100 a week and the government takes 350 to feed your lazy, unemployed drug addicts. Look at these guys, busting their asses in the sun. It's 107 Fahrenheit, it was just 115. Look at these guys flooring a mile a minute. What rapists and criminals?

CAMERAMAN: What drugs do you use?

LABOURER: My drug is this you son-of-a-bitch (holding up a mallet and hammer). This is my drug and this is my drink.

TRUMP SUPPORTER: He's one of us. He may be a millionaire which separates him from everyone else but he's still one of us.

MATT FREI: The British still think of Donald Trump as a bit of a joke. A punch line with a dodgy hairdo. But what does his candidacy and his success so far tell us about the state of our closest ally?[57]

ANN COULTER[58]: I was dubious about him until he started talking about Mexican rapists. Then I thought 'that's my guy!'. It is the most magnificent political document since the Magna Carta: Donald Trump's immigration policy paper.

JOHN OLIVER: At this point, Donald Trump is America's back mole: It may have seemed harmless a year ago, but now that it's gotten frighteningly bigger, it is no longer wise to ignore it.

CLINTON: I no longer think he's funny.

CRUZ: (soothingly, to Donald) Breathe. Breathe. Breathe. You can do it, you can breathe! I know it's hard, I know it's hard, but just –

RUBIO: When they're done with the yoga, can I answer a question?

ROMNEY: His promises are as worthless as a degree from Trump University. He's playing members of the American public for suckers: He gets a free ride to the White House, and all we get is a lousy hat.

CRUZ: Falsely accusing someone of lying is itself a lie and something Donald does daily.

RUBIO: He's calling me "Little Marco" and I'll admit the guy is taller than me, he's like 6'2", which is why I don't understand why his hands are the size of someone who's 5'2". Have you seen his hands? ... And you know what they say about men with small hands.

YOUTUBE USER: This country is fucked no matter who gets elected, if Trump gets elected at least we can get a good bit of entertainment while we're going down the shitter.

TRUMP: Show me someone without an ego and I'll show you a loser.

TRUMP: When people are in a focussed state, the words 'I can't', 'I'll try', 'I'll do it tomorrow' and 'maybe' get forced out of their vocabularies.

TRUMP: There is an old German proverb to the effect that 'fear makes the wolf bigger than he is' and that is true.

The Trump Freedom Jam (from a Donald Trump Rally in Pensacola, Florida)

Main Voice	*Second Voice*
Cowardice	are you serious?
Apologies for freedom	I can't handle this!
When freedom rings	answer the call!
On your feet	stand up tall!
Freedom's on our shoulders	USA!

Enemies of freedom, face the music Come on boys, take 'em down!

(in unison)
President Donald Trump goes out
to make America great

Deal from strength or get crushed every time
Over here   USA!
Over there   USA!
Freedom and liberty everywhere

(in unison)
Oh say can you see
It's not so easy
But we have to stand up tall
And answer freedom's call

USA   USA!
USA   USA!
We're the land of the free and the home of the
brave,
USA   USA!

(unison)
The stars and stripes are flying
Let's celebrate our freedom
Inspire proudly freedom to the world

I'm married to   USA!
American pride   USA!
It's attitude, it's who we are, stand up tall

(unison)
We're the red, white   Fiercely free,
And blue   that's who!
And our colours don't run,
No siree!

(dancing interlude)

Over here   USA!
Over there   USA!
Freedom and liberty everywhere

(unison)
Oh say can you see
It's not so easy
But we have to stand up tall and
Answer freedom's call
(end on salute)

OBAMA: I continue to believe that Mr Trump will
not be president. And the reason is because I have
a lot of faith in the American people. And I think
they recognise that being president is a serious job.
It's not hosting a talk show or a reality show. It's not
promotion. It's not marketing. It's hard. And a lot of
people count on us getting it right. it's not a matter

of pandering and doing whatever will get you in the news on a given day. Sometimes it requires you making hard decisions even when people don't like it.

AFTERWORD

TRUMP: Sadly, the American dream is dead.

AUDIENCE MEMBER: Bring it back.

TRUMP: But if I get elected president I will bring it back bigger and better and stronger than ever before, and we will make America great again.

Thank you. Thank you very much.

(APPLAUSE)

I'm well aware that this book does not carry the moral agenda many feel is now Trump's due. As the presidential race progressed he moved from a figure of controversy to a figure of hate and if I have not overemphasised what many think is most important about Trump – his power as a demagogue and his danger as a political figure – it is because that aspect of him is bound to be covered elsewhere[59]. Besides, it was far more interesting to look at the Trump that existed before his opponents and champions finalised his characterisation. Trump is a figure in our midst and, like all of us, he is open to interpretation. An historical figure, especially a well known one, is seen as through a telescope from a single angle. It is telling that when Trump is compared to Hitler, Mussolini or George Wallace, as he often is, the comparison sheds more light on his antecedents than on him. Trump serves as a present-day deconstruction of these political mythologies, for as Trump's political importance increases, the ways we are allowed to look at him decrease until he ceases to be a historical possibility and becomes a historical fact. With societal fractures as big as the ones Trump is at the epicentre of, we get forced to take one side or the other. This adds a layer of obscurity on top all the other obscurities and assumed truths that political discourse imposes on us.

The more we simplify events, the less able we are to interpret accurately or react effectively to phenomena like Trump. Interpretation of Trump's image and rhetoric is something that should belong to us, not to the mass opinion that buffets both him and us. Trump's weakness, his tragic flaw, is that he is not able to see beyond what his self-image and his media image make him out to be. We do not need to share that flaw.

ENDNOTES

0 Stokols, Eli. "Inside Jeb Bush's $150 Million Failure". *Politico.* February 20, 2016.

1 Documentary 'Life Story of Billionaire Donald Trump' characterises Fred as 'a builder' – endowing the Trumps with a fake kind of working class romanticism.

2 Narrator, 'Life Story of Billionaire Donald Trump'.

3 According to Trump's biographer in, 'The Mad World Of Donald Trump', Channel 4 documentary.

4 Narrator, 'Life Story of Billionaire Donald Trump'.

5 Narrator, 'Life Story of Billionaire Donald Trump'.

6 Zakaria, Fareed. 'Dear Donald Trump: China, Japan and Mexico are not 'killing us". *Washington Post*, September 17, 2015.

7 Lee, Brianna. 'Mexico's Drug War'. *Council On Foreign Relations,* March 5, 2014.

8 Speaking in Illinois. Video compliment of CSPAN. https://www.youtube.com/watch?v=AQxHmrm83M0

9 same source as above.

10 Andrew Rosenthal. 'So This is The Humbled Trump'. Blog post, *NY Times,* February 1, 2016 .

11 Haberman, Maggie 'Super Tuesday Takeaways: Trump and Clinton Sprint, While Others Stumble'. *The New York Times*, March 2, 2016.

12 comparisons made by David Remnick, editor of The New Yorker, Nicholas Kristof, columinst for the New York Times, comedians Bill Maher and Louis CK, and quoted in Bryant, Nick. 'Could Trump's vulgarity cost him the election?'. *BBC News*, March 8, 2016.

13 Carter, Graydon. 'Why Donald Trump will always be a 'short-fingered vulgarian". *Vanity Fair*, October 7, 2015. 'I took to referring to him as a 'short-fingered vulgarian' in the pages of *Spy* magazine. That was more than a quarter of a century ago. To this day, I receive the occasional envelope from Trump.

There is always a photo of him – generally a tear sheet from a magazine. On all of them he has circled his hand in gold Sharpie in a valiant effort to highlight the length of his fingers. I almost feel sorry for the poor fellow because, to me, the fingers still look abnormally stubby.'

14 Harvard Business School Professor Gerald Zaltman, interviewed by Manda Mahoney on the HBS website: 'Probing the unconscious mind of the consumer has tremendous value'.

15 Stray, Jonathan 'How much influence does the media really have over the elections? Digging into the data' *Nieman Lab*, January 11, 2016.

16 John Rawls, *Political Liberalism.* New York ; Chichester: Columbia University Press, c1993.

17 Robert Nozick. *Anarchy, State and Utopia*. Oxford: Blackwell, 1974. 'Taxation of earnings from labor is on a par with forced labor'.

18 Rick Wilson, Republican Media Consultant, speaking on MSNBC's 'All In With Chris Hayes'.

19 Dougherty, Michael Brendan. 'How an obscure adviser to Pat Buchanan predicted the wild Trump campaign in 1996'. *The Week*, January 19, 2016.

20 Samuel Francis, 'From Household to Nation'. Retrieved from http://www.unz.org/Pub/Chronicles-1996mar-00012.

21 Buchanan, in turn, advised presidents Nixon, Ford and Reagan.

22 Taub, Amanda. 'The rise of American authoritarianism'. *Vox*, March 1, 2016.

23 Contrast Chris Christie's later endorsement of Trump, after which he was mocked mercilessly for staring at the back of Trump's head during his Super Tuesday news conference. 'Chris Christie spent the entire speech screaming wordlessly. I have never seen someone scream so loud without using his mouth before ... His were the eyes of a man who has gazed into the abyss, and the abyss gazed back, and then he endorsed the abyss'. Petri, Alexandra. 'Chris Christie's wordless screaming'. *The Washington Post*, March 2, 2016.

24 Cillizza, Chris. 'Sarah Palin's rambling, remarkable and at times hard to understand endorsement of Donald Trump'. *The Washington Post*, January 20 2016.

25 Jason Johnson, *Political Consultants and Campaigns: One Day To Sell.* Boulder, Colo.: Westview Press, c2012.

26 Dzierzak, Lou. 'Factoring Fear, What Scares Us and Why'. *Scientific American,* October 27, 2008.

27 Roland Barthes 'The Death of the Author'. Retrieved from http://www.tbook.constantvzw.org/wp-content/death_authorbarthes.pdf on 03/2/16

28 as above

29 Populations and Samples: the Principles of Generalisation, author unknown. Retrieved from http://www.cios.org/readbook/rmcs/ch05.pdf on 03/02/16.

30 Trump on 'Meet The Press'. Retrieved from https://www.youtube.com/watch?v=s1B-okG3548 on 03/02/16.

31 'Donald, what time is it?' 'I can tell you because I own the biggest, most luxurious watch in the world'. Phillip Bump, *Washington Post*.

32 Brooks, David. 'Donald Trump isn't Real'. *New York Times,* February 2, 2016.

33 Trump on 'Meet The Press'. Retrieved from https://www.youtube.com/watch?v=s1B-okG3548 on 03/02/16.

34 Trump interviewed by NBC, 07/08/15. Retrieved 03/2/16 from https://www.youtube.com/watch?v=jk0Rl46dyK8.

35 Source: Politifact. http://www.politifact.com/personalities/donald-trump/statements/byruling/false/.

36 Holan, Angie Drobnic and Qiu, Linda. '2015 Lie of the Year. the campaign misstatements of Donald Trump'. *Politifact.* December 21, 2015.

37 Finkelstein, Mark 'ABC News: Hillary 'May Have Been Right' – 'Predicted' ISIS would use Trump in Video'. *Newsbusters.org*, January 2, 2016.

38 Fund, John. 'Trump's Call to Kill Family Members of Terrorists Is Quarter Baked'. *National Review*, December 18, 2015.

39 Cortellessa, Eric. 'Ex-ADL chief: Trump's 'raise your hand' gambit was deliberate, Nazi-style 'fascist gesture''. *Times of Israel*. March 7, 2016.

40 Milbank, Dana. 'Trump's flirtation with fascism'. *The Washington Post*. March 7, 2016

41 From Trump's June 16 announcement speech.

42 Consider that this book, too, mainly sources mainstream media.

43 Gray, Freddy. 'The Trump Phenomenon'. *The Spectator*. January 23, 2016.

44 As above.

45 Montgomerie, Tim. 'Lashing out in all directions'. *The Spectator,* January 23, 2016.

46 Bryant, Nick. 'US election 2016: Trump wins Mississippi, Michigan and Hawaii'. *BBC News*, March 9, 2016.

47 Pasick, Adam. 'The Trump campaign displays raw 'Trump meat' as he racks up more primary wins'. *Quartz*, March 8, 2016. The display of 'Trump meat' and red wine is Trump's version of Christ's transubstantiation. Given that 'Trump Steaks' were discontinued due to poor sales almost immediately after their launch in 2007, their meaning on the podium can only be symbolic.

48 Trump's Wikipedia page. Retrieved 03/02/16.

49 Johnson, Will and D'Antonio, Michael. 'Trump's Campaign is Damaging his Brand'. *Politico*, January 11, 2016.

50 Brad Pitt, Christian Bale and Ryan Gosling as hedge fund managers in *The Big Short*.

51 Trump, quoted in *Social Networking for Authors: Untapped Possibilities for Wealth* (2009) by Michael Volkin, p. 60.

52 Trump, quoted in Scott, Eugene. 'Trump believes in God, but hasn't sought forgiveness'. *CNN Politics*, July 19, 2015.

53 Jacobs, Ben. 'Donald Trump calls Pope Francis 'disgraceful' for questioning his faith'. *The Guardian*, February 18, 2016.

54 Kinsley, Michael. 'The Serious Problem with Treating Donald Trump Seriously'. *Vanity Fair*, November 2015.

55 Blow, Charles M. 'Demagogue for President'. *NY Times*, March 3, 2016.

56 lyrics to 'Snake' by Al Wilson. Ironic.

57 http://www.channel4.com/programmes/the-mad-world-of-donald-trump/on-demand/63576-001

58 conservative commentator in Matt Frei's Channel 4 documentary 'The Mad World Of Donald Trump'.

59 For instance, in David Brooks' rather brilliant opinion piece "No, Not Trump, Not Ever", *The New York Times*, March 18, 2016.